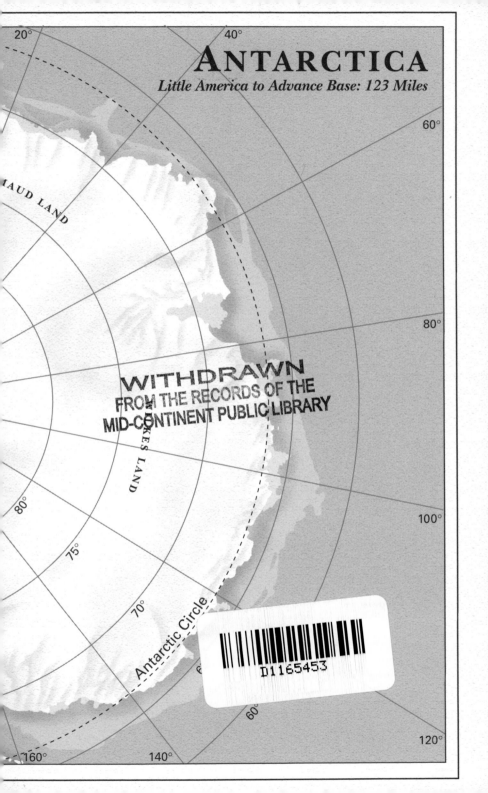

ANTARCTICA
Little America to Advance Base: 123 Miles

20°
40°
60°
80°
100°
120°
140°
160°

MAUD LAND

WILKES LAND

80°
75°
70°

Antarctic Circle

ADMIRAL RICHARD BYRD
ALONE IN ANTARCTICA

Admiral Richard Byrd

ADMIRAL RICHARD BYRD
ALONE IN ANTARCTICA

PAUL RINK

STERLING PUBLISHING CO., INC.
New York

A FLYING POINT PRESS BOOK

Design: PlutoMedia
Front cover photograph: PictureQuest
Back cover and frontispiece photograph: Byrd Polar Research Center
Archival Program, Ohio State University

Library of Congress Cataloging-in-Publication Data Available

2 4 6 8 10 9 7 5 3 1

Published by Sterling Publishing Co., Inc.
387 Park Avenue South, New York, NY 10016
Original edition published by Encyclopedia Britannica Press under the title
Richard E. Byrd: Conquering Antarctica. Copyright ©1961 by Paul Rink
New material in this updated edition
Copyright © 2006 by Flying Point Press
Maps copyright © by Sophie Kittredge, Creative Freelancers, Inc.
Distributed in Canada by Sterling Publishing
c/o Canadian Manda Group, 165 Dufferin Street
Toronto, Ontario, Canada M6K 3H6
Distributed in the United Kingdom by GMC Distribution Services
Castle Place, 166 High Street, Lewes, East Sussex, England BN7 1XU
Distributed in Australia by Capricorn Link (Australia) Pty. Ltd.
P.O. Box 704, Windsor, NSW 2756, Australia

Sterling ISBN-13: 978-1-4027-3189-1
ISBN-10: 1-4027-3189-2

For information about custom editions, special sales, premium and
corporate purchases, please contact Sterling Special Sales
Department at 800-805-5489 or specialsales@sterlingpub.com.

CONTENTS

ADMIRAL RICHARD BYRD
ALONE IN ANTARCTICA

CHAPTER 1

ADVENTURE AHEAD

SIX A.M., DECEMBER 2, 1928, DUNEDIN, NEW ZEALAND.

"Cast off forward!"

"Let go aft!"

Quick hands among the crowd on the dock loosed the lines from the bits. Bright yellow Manila moorings streaked through the dirty harbor water and were hauled dripping aboard the sailing ship *City of New York*.

The ship drifted away from the pier in the gentle tide. An old deep-water man stared at the vessel across the widening strip of water. The plimsoll line, a series of markings on the hull of a ship which tells how deeply she may be safely loaded, was far under water. The *City* was heavy with the burden of equipment necessary to support an exploring expedition through many months of an Antarctic night.

"You'll ship green water with every roll," the old man yelled prophetically.

The men crowding the *City*'s decks looked back without comment.

"You don't know what weather is until you work down into the sixties and seventies," came the creaking old voice again.

"Don't worry about us, Grampa," someone shouted back. "See you a year from now!"

Captain Frederick Melville signaled the skipper of the tugboat and slowly the *City* slipped down the narrow channel which leads from Dunedin to the sea. The *Eleanor Bolling*, the other ship of the expedition, followed under her own power.

Off Tairoa Head, the tug cast her tow loose and the ancient windjammer was free, trembling and throbbing under the massive surge of the ocean sweeping up to meet her.

Now Captain Brown of the *Bolling* threw across a quarter-inch steel towing rope, and it was made fast to the bow of the *City*.

The engine room telegraph of the *Bolling* swung to "Full Ahead," and slowly the two vessels gathered way, buckling down to the long voyage which lay ahead.

A lithe, slender man of 40 stood on the poop deck of the *City of New York* and gazed forward over the heaving, plunging length of the vessel. He gazed into the sea-scud and mists ahead, for somewhere out there lay the magic and wonder of a dream which he would make come true.

There are places and names of enchantment on this earth, places which draw our hearts and our spirits like magnets. Those who dream hard enough and are lucky enough, go to them. Ahead of Richard Evelyn Byrd—Admiral Byrd—now lay the last great unknown—the Antarctic. Tightly gripped in solid ice, the Antarctic was an enormous, savage, white wilderness, hostile, battered by howling hurricanes and blizzards.

Less was known about this 5 million square mile continent than of the surface of the moon. Here was a place which would resist man with every ounce of its awesome fury. Here was a rampart for a man to assault with every bit of strength in his body and spirit.

There were adventure and dreams enough for anyone, but between Byrd and their realization, lay grim reality. A thousand miles of storm-tormented ocean stretching to the south stood between him and a vital rendezvous with the Norwegian whaler *Larsen*, whose captain had volunteered to tow them through the ice pack. Once through the pack, supplies would have to be unloaded on the great ice barrier, and then, finally, winter quarters would have to be hollowed out of the steely glacial ice. The long Polar night would have to be endured, and then, when the sun once again threw its pale light over the Antarctic, perhaps the dream might be brought to flower.

With Captain Melville, and with Dr. Lawrence Gould, the geologist and second-in-command of the expedition, Byrd made a hurried survey of the tiny vessel.

Fifty-three men, nearly 100 sled dogs and about 500 tons of supplies and equipment were aboard. In the stern race to meet the *Larsen*, the gear had literally been dumped aboard.

Above decks and below, in the utmost confusion, were piled thousands of boxes and crates. Food for men and dogs, furs, canvas, clothing, gasoline, coal, scientific instruments, radio equipment, parts for airplanes—the list was endless. To get from forward to aft it was necessary to climb over this mountainous mass of cargo.

At the end of her towline, the overloaded vessel sluggishly rose and fell on the long, rolling waves. There was power in these great seas—latent, ominous power that could destroy the ship.

If the ship were to survive, if the dire prophecy of the old man on the dock in Dunedin were not to come true, room must be made for the men to work the vessel. And this must be done quickly for the southern oceans wait for no one.

The crew of the *City*, and the expedition members alike, were organized into port and starboard watches. Four hours on and four off, with little chance for sleep during off-duty hours below.

All hands set to work—sailors, scientists, and officers. Banks were emptied, the galley was set shipshape, passages and ladders were cleared, and the deck cargo securely lashed.

None too soon! As the days passed, the pulse of the weather quickened. At times the wind hauled to the north and the *City* was able to cast off her towline. Under the drive from her sails and the thrust of her tiny 200-horsepower engine, she drove through the making seas. Then, when the wind shifted, as it did without warning in these latitudes, sails were furled and the ship crept back to the safety of the *Bolling*'s towline.

Often the *City of New York* rolled her gunwales under. Green water swamped the decks, and Byrd was fearful that even the well-lashed boxes and crates would be swept overboard. Most of the men were greenhorns and suffered terribly from seasickness. Working on the towering masts and spars, high over the hissing sea was a new—and frightening—experience for these landlubbers.

The men who steered had perhaps the worst job of all. The wheel was exposed on the poop deck and it was necessary to keep at least two men on it at all times. Often two men were not enough. The force of the great seas on the rudder sometimes wrenched the wheel from their hands, spinning it wildly, and throwing the helmsmen across the deck.

As the weather increased, Byrd went forward one afternoon to observe the play of the two ships. Ahead, the *Bolling* rolled and pitched ponderously; under him the *City* gyrated madly, groaning in every seam and joint. Aloft the masts and spars clashed and creaked alarmingly. The towline slacked and tightened with quick jerks, and he knew it was only a question of time until it parted.

Back in the radio shack, writing out the order for the *Bolling* to cast them loose, he felt the vessel take a mighty plunge, then rise and shudder from stem to stern, as the towline bridle snapped. They were on their own. Sails were set and the engine started.

Early on a Sunday morning, a bit over a week since leaving Dunedin, there came a loud cry from a look-out on the masthead. "Ice ho! . . ."

Sverre Strom, one of the Norwegian ice pilots had sighted the first great guardian of the Antarctic. A huge iceberg. More came into view until they formed an endless procession, from one horizon to the other.

As the ships approached the ice, the ceaseless bedlam of ocean and wind noises was accompanied by the eery howling of the dogs. These Huskies, all of them from Alaska and Newfoundland, had spent many days chained in their cages, wet and miserable. Now, with the biting scent of ice in the air, they lifted their noses and unleashed their greeting to the gray skies. The sea, the tropics, the continual dampness had all been strange to them, but ice they knew and loved. Their work was close at hand and they were eager to be at it.

Somewhere ahead of them, the *Larsen* was prowling the edge of the ice pack, looking for an opening through which she could pass into the clear waters of the Ross Sea beyond. Here she would find her summer whale hunting.

Poor visibility made star sights nearly impossible to take. Consequently, neither Byrd's small fleet nor the *Larsen* knew exactly where they were. The rendezvous was going to be a difficult one.

In the radio shack, Byrd, Gould, and Captain Melville considered a message they had just received from Captain Nilsen, master of the whaler. The pack showed signs of breaking up, and he hoped to find a lead through it in a day or so.

Byrd looked out the porthole. In the sky was a vague, confused, gray-white reflection. Ice-blink, the reflection of the solid ice pack against the gray of the clouds. He looked at Dr. Gould.

"Time's almost run out, Larry."

Larry Gould nodded somberly. "That's right, Dick."

"How far do you estimate our position from that of the *Larsen*?" Byrd asked Captain Melville.

Melville shrugged. "Possibly a hundred miles. Maybe less. The trouble is, Dick, they don't know their exact position and—"

Byrd interrupted. "And we don't know ours. Like two needles in a haystack. Both lost!"

"Suppose we do have to fish around a bit? Won't Nilsen wait a day or two for us?"

Byrd threw Melville a glance and laughed shortly. "Sure. He'll wait. . . for $30,000 a day. Their season's short you know, and that's what they'll lose each day we keep them from their hunting. We don't have that kind of money. This expedition's already scraped the bottom of the barrel."

Byrd turned to the radio operator. "Sparks, keep at it. We've got to get a radio-compass bearing on the *Larsen*.

The man smiled. "Right, Sir. We'll pick her up."

Late that night, radio bearings from the whaler were established, and the *City* headed in her direction, followed by the *Bolling*. The huge masses of ice forced them to change course repeatedly. They had to be especially careful not to be caught for an instant in the edges of the main pack itself. The stout wooden sides and the design of the *City*'s hull could have withstood the pressure, but the steel plates of the *Bolling* would have been squeezed and crushed like the sides of a sardine can.

The ice pilots, Strom and Johanssen, spent long watches in the rigging keeping the ship out of trouble spots. Byrd and Captain Melville carefully steered the rugged *City of New York*, with the *Bolling* at their heels, in the direction of the whaler. Finally word floated down from the barrel lookout on the masthead.

"*Larsen* ho . . .!"

The gigantic whaler was riding safely in the distance, on the other side of a huge ice field.

Byrd and Melville studied the situation. By turning east the field could be safely passed. A few hours later the two ships rose and fell gently in an ice-locked harbor in the middle of the pack. A short distance away the great hull of the 17,000-ton whaler *Larsen* dominated the little bay.

There was no rest now for the members of the expedition. The *Bolling* had aboard her over 100 tons of badly needed coal which must be transferred to the *City of New York*.

The two ships were gingerly brought alongside each other. And now, the ocean's perverse temper gave them a touch of its malice. The coal transfer was started in a rising wind and sea. After several davits had been smashed and pieces of railing had been torn and splintered, Byrd called a halt. Sooner or later, a disastrous hole would have been smashed in the side of one or the other of the wildly diving and rolling ships.

At this tense moment, Sparks approached Byrd. "Message from the *Larsen*, Sir," he said, handing him the paper.

Byrd read it. His jaw tightened. He handed it to Gould. The message was from Captain Nilsen. "Expect to force the pack tonight or early tomorrow morning."

Byrd looked at Gould. There was deep concern in his eyes. "Larry, we've got to have that coal," he said quietly.

Gould couldn't even answer. The coal was not only necessary for the boilers of the *City*, but they were depending upon it to keep them warm on the ice during the winter which lay ahead. Mutely, Gould looked across the water to the wildly heaving *Bolling*. Impossible to transfer coal in this kind of a sea.

Byrd strode quickly to the radio shack, picked up the radiotelephone. "Captain Brown, please."

A moment later came the voice of the skipper of the heavily laden *Bolling*.

"Sir?"

"Captain, follow us into the shelter of the ice field."

The other man objected. "We may never be able to get back here, Dick," he said.

Brown was an old friend entitled to an explanation. "We'll have to risk it. The choice is simple. We've got to have the coal and we've got to be ready to leave with the *Larsen*."

Brown's "Aye, aye" was lost in the flurry of orders as the two ships got under way.

As Byrd suspected, in the protection of the ice field, they encountered long, powerful swells but none of the disastrous surface chop which made it so dangerous to bring the two ships together.

After two hours of careful maneuvering through the ice, Brown was able to tie his vessel alongside the *City of New York*. Soon all hands were on deck, transferring coal. All night they worked, in the thin glare of the midnight sun, and by eleven o'clock next morning the job was done.

After quick good-byes, and good-lucks, the *Bolling* set course back for Dunedin where she would reload, and make another trip with supplies for the expedition before the freezing Antarctic winter descended.

The tiny *City* crept cautiously back into the ice-harbor and settled down to await passage through the ice pack.

And now, the god of the Antarctic, perhaps more than

anything else to demonstrate the capriciousness of his moods, gave them a much needed break. The ice pack delayed the start of its breakup for another twenty-four hours. This gave the exhausted crew of the *City* a chance for some desperately needed rest. Very few of the company had had sufficient sleep for the past three days.

The *City of New York* had been built in Norway in 1882 for work with the sealing fleet which operated in the Arctic ice packs. Although very small—barely 170 feet in length—her size was deceptive. Gigantic strength had been built into her. Her original builders had named her the *Samson*, and the name was completely appropriate. Her oaken ribs were set so close together that a man could not get his hand between them. Inside she was sheathed with a heavy layer of virgin spruce. Outside was a layer of oak planking and on top of that still another layer of solid greenheart.

All told, her sides were 34 inches thick to help her withstand the direct, crushing pressure of ice. In addition, her hull had been cunningly designed so as to offer encircling ice no spot to seize her: she was rounded in such a way that the deadly embracing ice would lift the ship upward, instead of crushing her.

The enormous strength stood the stout little ship in good stead as she followed the *Larsen* into the pack. The procession of ships was a strange one. First came the *Larsen*, probing, pulling, widening the black hole through the ice. Then, at the end of a three-and-a-half-inch cable was the *City of New York*. When the *Larsen* dug in and pulled with all her strength, something had to give, and it was tricky work for those in the *City* to keep in line.

Behind the *City*, cautiously picking their way through the ice, which ever tended to close up again after the passage of the other two ships, followed the two small "killer," or chaser, boats which belonged to the whaler. They came under their own power, and often, as if in desperation, they drove themselves out of the water, threw themselves on the ice headlong, and broke it under their own weight before it could close in and lock them hopelessly.

Slowly the convoy pressed southward. Try as they would, the men on the *City* could not always avoid the great masses of ice which closed in behind the *Larsen*. They grew accustomed to the wrenching crashes, to the great masses of disturbed and scarcely balanced sheets of ice sliding slowly past—some of them as sheer and clean as though they had been cut by a saw. And always the creaking, the groaning, the grinding of the ice on the timbers—and the whispering shriek as it slowly rubbed its way along the sides of the ship.

At last, after ten nerve-wracking days, there appeared another kind of a blink in the sky, a gentle darkening of the horizon. Open water—the Ross Sea.

They soon cast off the towline. After a parting gift of whale meat—old whale for the dogs and young whale for the men—the *Larsen* set about her real business. The last glimpse the men on the *City* had of their good friend was the mighty bulk of the whaler looming against the white of the ice, close on the track of a plunging whale.

The dark waters of the Ross Sea were as smooth as a millpond, as the *City of New York*, under sail and steam, headed farther south.

CHAPTER 2

BUILDING LITTLE AMERICA

BYRD STOOD IN THE PROW OF THE SHIP AS SHE
sailed over the water toward the mystery and romance of the
vast Antarctic. Perhaps the tremble and eager surge of the hull
reminded him of another . . . a long time ago.

A slender, 13-year old stood before his father, a lawyer in the
sleepy, tree-shaded Virginia town of Winchester.

"Father," he said, "If you forbid me to go, I shall obey you."
Here the young voice took on depth, maturity. "But I shall
never forgive you."

Who could resist such yearning, such eagerness in a son?
Soon after, young Dick Byrd left his family and headed for the
Philippines to visit an old family friend, Judge Carson.

The United States Army Transport *Sumner* departed from San Francisco on a great circle course for Manila. In her bows Dick Byrd leaned against the rail and gazed westward. The first flying fish skittered in alarm from the foaming forefoot of the vessel, and the breeze carried with it the promise of heat.

He found strange lands at the end of his journey, strange peoples, ways and customs far different than those of Virginia. And adventure? Fishing by torchlight from canoes on whispering reefs, long treks into the jungles. This was 1902, just after the Philippine insurrection, and young Byrd made patrols with the Constabulary into the interior, cleaning out pockets of bandits and die-hard insurgents.

Months later, he continued his journey around the world, to home. The British tramp SS *Strathford* visited Borneo, Sarawak, Singapore, Colombo, Madagascar, Gibraltar, and many more fascinating places.

He soaked all the enchantment and mystery into the fibers of his being, but he wrote in his journal the sober, critical day-to-day chronicle of reality. A discussion of a book he was reading, Caesar's *Gallic Wars*; the coal consumption of the ship's boilers; astute comments on the life and politics of the lands he visited; notes on navigation.

He had a burning, overwhelming desire to know, and he lived forever after under its spell. Why must he see what lay beyond the mountains, the horizons, the seas? Why? How is any man to know the answer to this? Enough to say that Richard Byrd was a man and that the unknown was enough to stir his heart and set him to answering its call with all his heart.

The years when he was growing into manhood were filled with excitement and action, preparation and plan. Nothing was left to chance and if fate did intervene and a detour became necessary, the plans were changed, but the direction, never.

From the Virginia Military Institute, Byrd went into Annapolis and from there, of course, into the Navy. When a broken, improperly healed foot denied him the life of a line officer, he begged off his job as a desk officer and went to Pensacola to learn to fly.

In the old flying boats of those days, he became an accomplished aviator. Designing a new type of sextant, which substituted a bubble for the horizon, he pioneered in taking the rickety flying machines—little more than patched together affairs of canvas and wood—out of sight of land and navigating them safely home.

Shortly after the end of World War I he set up and planned the record-breaking flight of the NC Flying Boats which spanned the Atlantic. Although it was impossible for him to accompany the planes he swallowed his disappointment, trained the crews in his navigational methods, and did everything possible to make the flights successful.

Later, he was the commanding officer of the Naval Aviation section of an expedition which set out to map and explore hitherto unknown areas of the Arctic. During this expedition he came to know for the first time the great frozen wastes of the North. The excitement and adventure he found there were burned deeply into him.

He resigned from the peace-time Navy and prepared for his own launching into the unknown. He and Floyd Bennett, another Navy man, set out from Spitzbergen, Norway, and flew across the North Pole, the first men to do so. They returned home to a roaring welcome and both were awarded the Congressional Medal of Honor. (Later, however, controversy arose over Byrd's claim to have reached the pole.)

But there was more than medals and honors and receptions in their minds. They had flown across the North Pole. Now they must try the South Pole!

Here fate intervened. Byrd's great love was flying, and he had a deep and abiding faith in the future of aviation. This was the crazy summer of 1927 when the "flying machine" was just coming out of its infancy. Planes and engines had become reliable enough for men to undertake long-distance sustained flights. This was the summer of Lindberg, Nungesser, Coli, Chamberlin, and others. Some of these men completed their flights; some of them staggered into the air in over-burdened planes and were never heard of again. But man was on his way into the skies! The oceans had been spanned; the world had become enormously shrunken in size.

Byrd believed that the future of aviation would belong to multi-engined planes. True, each engine increased the possibility of mechanical failure, but the load which the plane could carry was also increased. He set out with the crew across the Atlantic in a great tri-motor Fokker. They reached Paris, but because of heavy fog, could not land. They were forced to turn back and ditch the ship on the coast. On this trip, however, he proved the value of his contention. The *America* carried a huge amount of radio and navigational equipment in addition to over 800 pounds of pay load—the first ship to fly the Atlantic carrying more weight than that of the bare gasoline necessary to get to her destination.

Momentarily stunned by the sudden death of his closest companion, Floyd Bennett, who had contracted pneumonia while flying a mercy mission in Canada, Byrd now plunged into the final preparations for the trip to the Antarctic.

His life up to now had been filled with enough adventure and excitement to satisfy any ordinary man. But always the unknown was ahead, waiting . . . simply there. He could do no less than heed its challenge.

And now another challenge was before him. To meet this challenge would call for every ounce of his nerve, his brains, his courage.

It was Christmas of 1928 when he stood in the bow of the ship headed over the Ross Sea. Ahead, to the south, Byrd saw again an imperceptible brightening in the sky. The sullen gray-black of the clouds and the sea seemed to flicker, to scintillate gently. The ice-blink of the Ross Barrier beckoned in the sky.

The Ross Barrier is like nothing else on this earth. The last awesome remnant of the Ice Age on our planet, it is shaped like a huge arrowhead, the broad edge of which runs in a general straight east-west direction for about 400 miles. The point, or tip of the arrow lies about 400 miles southward, pointing directly to the South Pole. Half supported by the bottom of the Ross Sea, and half floating, it is an unbroken, flat-topped sheet of solid ice hundreds of feet thick.

Gigantic glaciers on the Polar Plateau, as well as other smaller glaciers along the sides, feed it continually with fresh ice and push it to the sea. The outer edge, pushed forward by the pressure of the glaciers behind, constantly crumbles and breaks under the violence of the sea, creating great bergs and fields of ice, some of which are more than forty miles long. This edge of the Barrier facing the sea is the source of most of the mighty icebergs which roam the southern oceans.

There were many places along the edge of the enormous, ice-shrouded continent where a landing could have been made, and a base for the expedition established. Byrd, however, had chosen the Ross Barrier for very good reasons. Since planes were going to be used for the dash to the pole as well as for a vast amount of aerial exploration and mapping, it was essential to have a base from which they could operate.

The surface of the Barrier, although pitted in many places with crevasses, and dotted with hills and valleys of ice and drift, was smooth enough in many areas so that a plane equipped with skis could land and take off. Furthermore, Raold Amundsen, the great Norwegian explorer who had been the first man to reach the South Pole, had been across this area in 1912 with dog sledges. He had assured Byrd that on the Barrier the winds were far less violent than on other parts of the vast continent, where hurricane velocities were common.

As the *City of New York*, under sail, ghosted silently over the water, the edge of the Barrier was an awesome and forbidding sight. The huge rampart, an enormous cliff of solid ice, crumbled, broke, changed shape before their eyes under the continual gnawing of the sea. It was pocked with fairyland caves; it split into fantastic chasms which like prisms, reflected in magnificent color the pale sun overhead. In some places this cliff was as low as 20 feet. In others it towered 150 feet, or more, into the sky.

Somewhere on this desolate field of ice a landing would have to be made. Tons upon tons of supplies—everything necessary to maintain a 20th century city of 40 men throughout the winter—must be unloaded. Then the city itself would have to be built, hollowed out of the living ice, the wooden shacks buried in deep pits, to prevent their being overwhelmed by the storms and blizzards which were expected during the long months of night which lay ahead.

All this must be done quickly, for the Antarctic summer is short. The days and hours and minutes were more precious than gold.

According to Shackelton and Amundsen, two great Antarctic explorers who preceded Byrd, the Bay of Whales was a huge indentation where the Ross Barrier dropped to within a few feet of the surface of the water. The area along this stretch would be ideal for unloading.

In one important aspect, however, the reports of the two men differed. According to Shackelton, the Bay of Whales was nothing more than an accidental, temporary indentation in the ice of the Barrier. According to Amundsen, the Bay was not accidental, nor temporary. He felt that the Bay was caused by the shallowness of the Ross Sea at this point. He believed that the seaward movement of the glacier was impeded and held back by solid earth underneath, that the ice here was not floating, but rested on the bottom. If this were true then conditions would be ideal not only for unloading but for the establishment of the city itself. The chances were very slight that the ice would break off and float out to sea!

"Sir," came a soft voice outside his cabin door. "Bay of Whales broad on the starboard bow."

Byrd hurried topside, and saw through the fog and mist the icy headlands. Slowly the ship crept forward. Byrd strained his eyes, peering for the broad opening of the Bay.

And then, his heart fell. There was the Bay all right, but it was choked with ice. Mile upon mile of heaving pressure ridges and tightly massed bergs made it out of the question for a ship even with a hundred times the power of the *City of New York* to force an entrance.

Reluctantly he gave the order to bring the vessel about.

"We'll moor alongside the Barrier outside the Bay," he instructed Captain Melville.

Soon the *City* slid cautiously alongside the bay ice of the Barrier. The landing party jumped ashore, moorings were sunk, and for the first time in months, the ship lay quiet, heaving and surging gently in the low swells.

Two dog teams, led by Byrd and Chief Pilot Bernt Balchen, prepared immediately to set out and find a suitable location for the city.

After an exploratory trip which lasted several days, they found an ideal spot. It was in a gentle hollow, with rims of snow to protect it from winds that might come from any direction but the West. Nearby were large smooth expanses which would serve as a landing field for the planes. The only drawback was its distance from the edge of the Barrier where the ship was moored. Byrd insisted on the location, even though it would make the unloading process somewhat drawn out. He wanted to take no chances on a break-up of the ice which might endanger Little America—for so the city was to be named.

In a fast changing kaleidoscope of time and motion, the next several months developed into a battle to unload and erect the base.

Decisions crowded one upon another. At times Byrd seemed literally crushed under the weight of responsibility. The *Bolling* was expected back in several weeks with additional supplies. She and the *City* must be unloaded before the return of winter and night. In addition, the construction of Little America had to be sufficiently advanced, so that the men would be housed as quickly as possible.

Byrd was everywhere, urging his men, welding them into a smooth, loyal, well-organized outfit.

So desperate was the race for time that he finally decided to establish an auxiliary base a short distance away from the Barrier edge. Equipment was rolled down wooden planks or winched onto the ice. From shipside it was man-hauled on sledges to his first cache and from there, loaded on dog sledges for the run to Little America.

The edge of the ice constantly crumbled and broke. Often it disintegrated so badly that the position of the ship had to be changed. Fortunately, no one was hurt or lost during these sudden breaks.

Everybody united in the common effort to unload—sailors, scientists, officers, fliers, stokers. Some days the unloading went well; there were others when for all their efforts, a miserable four tons were all they had to show for the work.

The dogs went insane with joy at their release from their cramped, wet cages on the ship. They hauled the loads like fiends, straining, stretched flat on their bellies, pulling with every muscle. Because of their long confinement they were at first unreliable. At some imaginary insult from a team-mate, they would fly at each other with fang and claw, until an entire team became a snarled, tangled mass of fighting dogs who could only be separated by the force of a heavy club—and then not until the precious sledge-load of supplies had been scattered and dropped along the trail.

Often the strength of the dogs was not enough. Men roped themselves to their teams. Often the trail lay across thinly bridged crevasses, which broke under the weight and left the men dangling over certain death. Hauled out by their comrades they nonchalantly carried on.

The base at Little America was a full nine miles away which meant that each round trip was a distance of eighteen miles. Little America during this period seemed as distant and inaccessible as the moon.

Then one day there came a cry from the lookout. A great crack had opened up on the Barrier; a huge piece had broken off. Swiftly the *City* was gotten underway and moved. She shoved her nose into the lead, nudged it open, and moved two miles closer to the Base.

The *Bolling* arrived with the balance of the supplies, and efforts were redoubled. The three planes were unloaded. First, the small, single-engine Fairchild, then a larger single-engined Fokker, and finally, the huge Ford tri-motor. The weight of the fuselage of the Ford was too much for the ice. Right after this great weight had been moved from the edge, the entire wall of the Barrier collapsed, burying the *City* and the *Bolling* under hundreds of tons of ice. The vessels careened, their keels rose dripping into the pale yellow sunlight. For long, terrible moments the two ships hung between safety and destruction, and then, as the ice slid ponderously across the steeply tilted decks, the vessels slowly righted themselves.

This was an agonizing experience. One man was left dangling in midair by a rope from the edge of the Barrier. He was hauled to safety. Two others were tossed overboard by the cascading ice. One of them nonchalantly paddled on a plank, and the other, who could not swim, drifted out of sight, with a chunk of ice for support under each arm! A whaleboat was swung out, launched, and both were rescued, although they suffered badly from their immersion in the freezing water.

Throughout all the unloading, the sea provided plenty of company for the men. Whales spouted near them. Killer whales, great Antarctic predators, ambushed and nearly attacked an exploratory party in one of the whaleboats. All kinds of seals swam about the ship or floated past on rafts of ice, gazing curiously at the intruders. Penguins—the great emperors and the smaller Adelies—bowed and made speeches of welcome. They investigated everything within reach—dogs, men, ships, supplies. Nothing could satisfy the curiosity of these charming and comical little creatures.

The work at Little America, under Larry Gould's direction, progressed amazingly well. Foundations were dug. Buildings were going up, the radio towers were being erected, storehouses constructed. But Byrd, on a morning tour of inspection found that some of the foundations were not deep enough. Many of the buildings already started would project more than half their bulk above the surface of the ice, making them too vulnerable to the storms of winter.

"Larry, that's not enough protection from the winter blizzards."

"It should be enough, Dick. The men are tired. We've got to get shelter for them, get them undercover."

"Sorry, Larry. They've got to be dug deeper. Better to be tired and cramped now than to run the risk of being blown off the Barrier in the dead of winter."

Another time deep, strong foundations had been dug for the administration building, but Byrd found to his horror that they were smack up against the already erected Mess Hall.

Should he order the foundations dug again? Do the work all over, two hundred yards away?" But why? Danger of fire. Fire, here on the frozen Barrier? Certainly. Put the buildings too close together, someone gets careless, knocks over a can of gasoline and the men would be without supplies or food.

So the weary men began digging another set of foundations in the steely ice.

If Byrd erred it was always in the direction of over-caution, of over-regard for the safety of his men. Behind him were years of experience and discipline which had taught him the bitter lesson that man is liable to error and since this is the case, it is better that his mistakes be in the direction of safety.

Soon the ships must be gone. The *Bolling* was unloaded and left for New Zealand with the hope that she would be able to make one more trip back to the Ross Barrier before the freeze set in. The effort was fruitless however, because by the time she returned, the ice pack had already started to close in. To attempt to get through would have meant her certain destruction.

Daily the sun dipped lower and lower, but still the work went on. A thousand things had to be attended to while there was still light.

As soon as men could be spared, Byrd organized a detail to lay in a supply of seal meat for the winter. Seals by the score lay sunning themselves on the floating ice and on the pressure field which jammed the Bay of Whales. Fat, sleepy, they offered no fight to the men who came to slaughter them. When approached, they opened their eyes, lazily grunted, and returned to their slumbers. A hard kick in the ribs scarcely caused them to stir. Feeling more like executioners than hunters, the men dispatched their victims with a quick, point-blank shot between the eyes. In this manner over a hundred tons of seal meat were gathered and laboriously hauled up the Barrier and stored in a meat house. This meat would feed the dogs during the winter, and would also be eaten by the men. It was excellent for the prevention of scurvy.

During all this driving period of getting settled, Byrd found time to make several flights, mapping and photographing parts of the vast, unknown continent. The purpose of the expedition was to increase man's store of knowledge; this was never forgotten. Byrd always did the navigating on these flights, taking only occasional relief tricks at the wheel of the plane. The sheer beauty of flight, and the shining, irrefutable logic of navigation had always been Byrd's great loves. On these trips especially, looking down on vast ice-sheathed mountains and valleys, never before seen by mortal eyes, the exhilaration felt by the explorer transcended all other feelings.

Near the end of February, the *City of New York* cast her moorings, and vanished into the sea smoke, bound for New Zealand, where she would winter. She was completely unloaded and had made several exploratory trips up and down the coast of the Barrier. But now the temperature was dropping far below zero. Pancake ice was forming on the surface of the water; in another few days the ship might have been solidly frozen in.

Every member of the crew of the *City* had struggled and worked desperately to set up the winter party and there was not one among them who did not cherish the secret hope of staying through the night on the Barrier. Two additional men, who could be spared from the work on the ship, were finally allowed to remain, increasing the party to 42. The others had to return. As Byrd stood on the poop deck of the ship, telling them good-bye, there was little he could say but . . . "Thank you." Perhaps the eloquence of silence achieved more than words could ever have done. The crewmen swallowed their disappointment and headed the vessel into the mists, toward the north.

CHAPTER 3

THE LONG WINTER NIGHT

FOR THE MEN WHO REMAINED BEHIND, THE GRINDING work continued. Many buildings had to be erected; tons and tons of supplies were still piled in jumbled masses along the edge of the Barrier and the trail. It all had to be hauled across the ice to the city.

With the passing of summer, the temperature plunged lower and lower. Storms, only hints of what might be expected later, howled down out of the great Polar Plateau to the south.

The city was finally all laid out; the carpenters were putting up the final buildings. Supplies were stored, and seal meat was laid in. Tunnels were hollowed out of the ice to connect all the buildings, so that the men could go from one to the other without having to venture on the surface.

Soon they would experience the long Polar night. This would be a time to relax, to plan, to organize equipment for the field expeditions next summer.

While the light lasted, there was exploratory work to be done. Four parties were sent out to establish supply depots to the south. Caches were set up at 20 miles, 40 miles, and 44 miles. The depots were well marked by flags, and among them were distributed 1,350 pounds of man and dog food, as well as equipment. Surveying parties were sent along the Bay of Whales to try to establish accurately its contours.

The time was growing late, however. The good weather was only intermittent now—sunshine was followed by darkness and squalls of wind and snow. Dr. Lawrence Gould, geologist for the expedition, approached Byrd for permission to make a short flight to the base of the nearby Rockefeller Mountains, a distance of about 125 miles. This vast range had been discovered on one of the exploratory flights.

Byrd reluctantly granted permission for the flight. Such a venture could be very dangerous. On the other hand, with a little luck, the men could pull it off. There was no denying that the geological survey was important. If it could be accomplished now, they would save much time next summer.

The Fokker shook its skis clear in a great cloud of snow and headed east. Dr. Gould was in command, Bernt Balchen was pilot, and Harold June served as radio man and co-pilot. About two hours later they reported a safe landing on a smooth ice field at the foot of the Rockefeller Mountains.

A series of blinding blizzards descended on Little America. In the midst of this bad weather, radio communication with Gould's party was cut off.

Five days passed. There was no word from the party. Byrd maintained constant vigil in the radio shack at Little America. Three more days went by—days of storm and plunging temperatures. Byrd was beside himself with worry and remorse. Against his better judgment, but swayed by the logical urging of his friends, he had given his permission for the flight. He resolved never again to go against his own instincts.

Plans were made to send out a dog rescue team, and to attempt rescue flights in the single engine Fairchild. Everyone waited abatement of the blizzard.

At last Bill Haines, the meteorologist, gave a conditional "all clear" for the rescue flight. "Dick," he said, "I can't answer for the weather this time of year. It might be calm here but blowing a blizzard a hundred miles away. You have one chance in three of making it."

One chance in three was good enough for Byrd. With Dean Smith as pilot, Hanson as radio man, and doing the navigating himself, Byrd took off. With difficulty they found the camp beside a huge landing "T" marked in the snow. The site was in the bottom of a great bowl. The landing conditions were tricky; the air was filled with milky and opaque mist, making it difficult to judge distance or height. Smith dropped the Fairchild in for a perfect landing and three men came running toward them from a little tent. All were safe.

What had happened? Wordlessly, Balchen and Gould pointed to the wreck of the Fokker a short distance away. Byrd strolled over to it. The blades of the propeller were curled like corkscrews, sure evidence of a power dive. He turned questioningly to Balchen.

"The gusts of wind in the blizzard reached 150 miles an hour," Balchen said.

This wind velocity was far more than necessary to give the Fokker a true flying speed. The wind had spun the propeller, and then torn the anchoring snow blocks and guy wires loose. With propeller spinning, the plane had flown backwards by itself, and crashed.

In relays, the party was flown back to Little America. From then on they were known as the "men who had been lost in the mountains." They insisted they had never been lost, but had known where they were at all times. The episode had been a near tragedy, and had cost the expedition an airplane.

Little America now settled down to the final business of going under the ice for the winter. The last supplies of seal meat were stored in the meat-house. The last supplies dumped on the edge of the Barrier were sledged into the city. The last houses were nailed together. The final connecting tunnels were hacked through the ice.

The wings on the Fairchild were folded back and the ship was eased into a large pit dug in the ice. Covered with snow, she would be safe for the winter.

The huge Ford tri-motor, christened the *Floyd Bennett*, was also prepared for winter. An enormous hole was dug in the ice, deep enough to take the entire fuselage, with just the tail projecting above the surface. Snow was shoveled and piled high over this so it would be safe from the wind. Another house made of snow blocks was built over the nose section, to form a sort of hangar where the mechanics could work on the engines. The wing was buried by itself some distance away.

The periods the sun stayed below the horizon were getting longer and longer. Finally, on April 22, the sun vanished for the winter.

Little America was buttoned up, sealed in, and prepared for the long months of darkness and cold.

The awesome might of the full Antarctic winter clamped its grip on the city. Stupendous blizzards roared down from the icy wastes, filling the air with shrieking sound, snow, and drift.

Temperatures dropped to 20, to 40, occasionally to 70 degrees below zero. The cold was so intense that a man's lungs burned and stung, and his breath snapped in the air like a string of firecrackers. Strong steel turned weak and brittle. Kerosene became like thick syrup, and flashlight batteries failed to deliver any electricity.

In periods of calm, when the men dared to venture out of their tunnels to the surface of the Barrier, the sky crackled and swarmed with stars. The air was clean, pure, without a trace of dust or mist. Twenty-four-hour darkness reigned, broken only by the flashing, scintillating, fading display of the aurora australis, or by the glow of the moon—now yellow, now green, now an unearthly blue.

Nothing lived on the Barrier but the 42 men of the expedition, huddled in their tunnels and in their huts, crouched about their stoves deep below the surface, far from the reach of the wind and storm. Forty-two men and ninety-five dogs patiently waited for spring to come when they could emerge again into light. Like hibernating animals, they waited. Many months were to pass before the sun would peek over the horizon and swing into the sky for the brief summer.

Unlike hibernating creatures, however, they could not pass the time simply sleeping and waiting. They were men, with all man's need for stimulation, entertainment and activity.

There was a library with over 3,000 books. Impromptu entertainments were staged. There was much talk, because above all other things, man is a communicating animal. Yarns were spun, stories told. Men probed each other in long hours of conversation, discovering things about each other—how they felt, what they thought.

The winter was not an easy time. Men became irritable; got on each other's nerves. There came times when one's best friend seemed dull, boring and downright annoying. There was no such thing as privacy in this rabbit warren of tunnels and cramped quarters. It is surprising that there was so little trouble. Perhaps it was because the men had learned to discipline themselves and to control their emotions. As the doctor of the expedition, Dana Coman, said, "I have found that the longer you know a man, the better you like him."

There was, of course, an eternal round of duties to be performed, all of them intensified and made far more difficult by the environment. Wisely, Byrd saw to it that each man in the city had some kind of work to perform.

A large number of men were occupied in the daily chores of housekeeping. The list of tasks was endless, and, in order that no man or group of men would be stuck with the less glamorous jobs, the chores were rotated. Everybody took a turn at assisting the cook, waiting on the mess table, washing dishes, sweeping, shoveling snow from the entrances, building fires in the stoves in the morning, bringing in coal, keeping the tunnels clear of debris, maintaining a night fire watch, and so on.

One never ending task was that of supplying the company with water. It might seem simple—living in a glacier! Actually it was not. The water necessary for cleaning, cooking, drinking, development of photographs, was a never-ending problem. It all had to be made by melting snow. Filling the large water buckets on the stoves kept a detail of men busy every day.

The dogs were chained in a separate tunnel called Dog Town. Each Husky had room enough to move about a bit and rub noses with his neighbor, but no more, or fearful fights and tangles would take place. The task of chopping up the frozen seal carcasses and serving each dog his daily allotment was a constant chore.

The lady members of Dog Town began producing litters of puppies that roamed like frisky young wolf cubs. They were great pets with the men, very friendly and playful. These hardy young pups, skittish as wild creatures, never came indoors, nor very rarely did they venture into what was for them very dangerous territory—the tunnels of Dog Town. They lived outdoors, on the surface of the Barrier through the fiercest storms, and never were animals more healthy!

In addition to the daily housekeeping jobs, there was scientific work to be done. This was a scientific expedition, very strongly staffed, wintering for the first time in history on the great ice barrier, literally within the shadow of the South Pole.

One of Byrd's primary concerns was the gathering of data about this strange country.

The huge ice cap at the bottom of the world is the source of the weather in the Southern Hemisphere. Storms, hurricanes, droughts, rain—all trace their origins to what is happening in the Antarctic. The great winds which blow out of the South toward the equator and then rise, heated, to return to the ice and snow again, constitute a kind of gigantic respiration of our earth. This colossal "breathing," many meteorologists believe, interlocks with similar winds coming down out of the Arctic.

Man is only beginning to fathom the mystery of the weather. For this reason, the daily records kept by Byrd's expedition were vital. This was the first orderly attempt ever made to collect knowledge at the heart of our weather system, the area around the South Pole.

Temperatures, barometric readings, humidity readings, and wind velocities were meticulously observed and tabulated. One of the coldest jobs of the expedition was to measure the upper wind currents. A hatch, like a small skylight, was made in the roof of the weather shack. From here, balloons filled with hydrogen were released. Their height and velocity were recorded by means of a theodolite, an instrument like a surveyor's sextant which measures angles. During the periods of darkness, small lighted candles were suspended beneath the balloons, so that the shivering observer, his eye glued to the ice-encrusted telescope of the theodolite, could track them. Often it was so cold that the candles would not light. They first had to be heated over a stove!

Byrd had proposed that by the arrival of the Antarctic spring, two important parties should be ready to take the field.

One, led by himself, would head the big Ford tri-motor due south for a flight over the Pole, mapping and photographing as they went. This meant a round trip from Little America of about 1,600 miles.

A second party, led by Dr. Gould, would also head due south, to the extreme end of the Ross Barrier and into the Queen Maud Mountains. The purpose of this party was to make a geological examination—the first ever attempted—of the land masses of Antarctica. Gould planned to be gone from Little America for about three months, during which time his party would cover about 1,500 miles. This distance would have to be made mainly on foot, as only rarely could they count on riding the sledges. The dogs had enough to do to pull food and equipment without the added weight of the men.

The problem of the fliers was to fit the performance of the plane to the job which it had to do. The plane would have to lift quite a bit of weight at the take-off: four men, navigational equipment, radios, cameras, gasoline, oil, emergency food in case of a forced landing, and so on. The first 400 miles would be across the Barrier, at relatively low altitude. At this point however, the plane would have to climb to 10,000 feet so as to clear the mountains and glaciers of the Queen Maud Range and get up over the Polar Plateau. What was the maximum weight the plane could carry and still attain this altitude? And still have enough gas to get to the Pole and then back to Little America? They finally decided to establish a gasoline dump at the foot of the mountains, where the ship could land and pick up fuel on the way home.

As Byrd and his plane crew grappled with the problems of fuel and load limits, so did Gould and his men struggle with their particular problems. In the Antarctic, time is everything. For the fliers, time was bought with gasoline. For the sledge party, time was brought with food.

An Antarctic expedition must carry with it every single ounce of food it expects to consume. It cannot even hope to meet an occasional animal or bird. A depot system, therefore, must be established. Starting out, the party has an extremely heavy load. As it travels along, it drops off in caches, usually a day's run apart, supplies of food for men and dogs. Homeward bound, following the same trail, which is marked every mile of the way with small orange flags mounted on bamboo sticks, the party is able to sustain itself. The problem, of course, is to decide how much to start off with and how much to leave off at each depot.

In addition to the daily calculated consumption, reserves over this bare minimum must be provided in case of delay. Since this was to be an extraordinarily long sledge journey, it would have been impossible for the teams at the start to have pulled enough to satisfy fully all the needs of the party. Accordingly, a supporting party was organized, which would go on ahead, establish depots for a distance of 200 miles, and return to Little America.

In addition to this, the geological party was to act as a rescue unit in case the Polar flight ran into trouble along the route. These demands had to be calculated into the overall planning.

The love which Polar explorers have for the gallant dogs

who pull the sledges is deep and abiding. However, the stern law of survival dictates other terms than those of sentiment. Explorers who expect to live cannot be swayed by any law other than that of the trail. As a trip progresses, the dogs that are worn out must be put to death. An actual table of expectancy is worked out. Fewer dogs means that less dog food has to be carried, but it also means that less weight can be pulled. These factors must be considered and balanced out very carefully. The geological party would start out with 5 teams of 9 dogs each, a total of 45. On their return to Little America, they expected to have only 3 teams of 7 dogs each, a total of 21; the others would have been sacrificed to the demands of stark necessity.

Many of the answers which the planners had to know during this period of preparation were unknown. Whenever possible, experiments were conducted.

What was the best type of cooker to provide half-frozen men with pemmican "hoosh", or soup, in the shortest possible time? A slow, or balky cooker, might mean the difference between life and death. After much trial, a new one was developed by the machinists at the base out of a basic type called a Nansen Cooker, after its inventor, Nansen, the great Arctic explorer.

What was the best type of tent? It must be light, strong, and large enough to shelter them from the blizzards which they were sure to encounter. Martin Ronne, the old Norwegian sail-maker, spent long weeks over his sewing machine before a final design was adopted.

How about sleeping bags? A night's rest for the men was imperative. Brave volunteers slept on the cold surface of the

Barrier testing different kinds before reindeer-skin bags were finally decided upon.

And how about the performance of the Ford tri-motor? A host of data was needed—far beyond that supplied by the manufacturer. Ceilings under various loads. Safe load capacity. Safe landing and take-off loads and speeds using skis. The proper design of skis for such a large plane was unknown. Fuel consumption literally down to the minute, under different conditions which they might encounter, must be determined. Byrd planned to run a series of test flights as soon as the winter was over.

Never had Byrd's genius for planning and his capacity for leadership been more clearly demonstrated than during this long night when the plans were being made. One of his great traits was his faith and belief in other men. Those with him had been carefully chosen; they were experts in their own fields. Under his guidance, they worked and solved most of their problems themselves.

When the men could not reach agreement, all the facts, including the minority views, were presented to Byrd, who then, after much thought, discussion, appraisal of the problem, and considerable soul-searching, gave his decision. Right or wrong, the decisions had to be made and it was upon his shoulders that the ultimate responsibility rested.

The night dragged on through the months to its appointed end. One day the sun peeked briefly over the horizon and then vanished, to return for a bit longer the following day. Activities in the camp reached a feverish pitch.

The real work of the expedition—the flight over the Pole, the mapping, the surveying, the geological examination of the great Queen Maud Mountains—must all be accomplished in the short spring and summer, before the return of the ships through the ice pack to take them home. Once again, time became the great enemy. Frantically, the men doled it out to themselves in days, hours, and minutes. None must be wasted.

CHAPTER 4

EXPLORING THE ICE BARRIER

BY THE FIFTEENTH OF OCTOBER, BOTH THE SUPPORTING party and the geological party were ready for the field. The weather was perfect for the start. Temperature was 10 degrees below zero, sky slightly overcast, with a gentle breeze from the northeast.

On a sledge drawn by a team of half-broken, unruly pups, that now were as big and powerful as their elders, Byrd accompanied the parties for a few miles across the smooth bay ice up to the ridge of the Barrier proper. Twice as many pups were pulling as were needed and the ride was a wild one. They sped like bullets past the heavily laden sledges of the main parties.

The loaded sledges at last caught up. The parting was brief. Byrd looked each man in the eye as they shook hands. He told them: "You can do it if any men can. Every man in camp is back of you with everything we have. The only thing I ask you to remember is that the life of any man is worth more than anything we can accomplish. That comes first. Good luck. Take the necessary precautions and you'll come back O.K. Now go to it."

With a cracking of whips and a shrill "Hi, Hi, Hi" to the dogs, the drivers urged their teams southward, into the vast, frozen unknown.

Byrd turned to Balchen, his chief pilot. "Bernt," he said, "The spirit of those men will never break. That I know."

"Right, Dick," echoed the tall Norwegian. "But their luck? Ah . . . that's something else. With good luck, men can do anything. With bad luck they can do nothing."

Byrd grinned briefly at his friend, but his glance turned somber as he stood looking at the long string of dogs, men, and sledges vanishing into the white glare beyond.

"I'm afraid," he said simply. "Too much weight on those sledges. Too many miles ahead of them."

His apprehensions were well grounded. Soon both parties were in serious trouble. They ran into heavy drifts and the dogs could not move the loads. The men stripped off their outer clothing and harnessed themselves to the sledges with their animals. After two days of heart-breaking work they had made only twenty miles. Men and dogs were utterly worn out.

After a series of hurried conferences on the trail, and by radio with Byrd back at the base, the geological party decided to return to Little America for reorganization. Meantime, the supporting party would continue with lighter loads.

Byrd addressed the men: "Antarctica begrudges everything but hardship. No single effort can overwhelm it. The work of the geological party is of greater importance than the purely geographical investigations of the aviation unit. If you fail, the work of the whole expedition will be the less for it. I do not propose to tell you how to lighten your loads. You will know how to do it better than I. But I do promise you every resource of the expedition to assist you."

He then characteristically left the matter in their hands. They would know better than he just what had given them trouble on the trail, and what must be done to overcome it. Byrd had full confidence in all of them. They were courageous, resourceful, and determined men.

By the 4th of November, the geological party, reorganized and toughened by their previous chastening experience, were ready for another start. The supporting party, having long since attained all its objectives would soon be back in Little America.

This time, the geological party made excellent daily runs and drove steadily southward into the heart of the Antarctic continent. As the encouraging reports came back by radio, Byrd was able to relax somewhat and turn his full attention to the next problem—the base-laying flight and the final dash for the South Pole in the Ford tri-motor.

The plane was as fit as human hands could make her. During the winter months she had been thoroughly gone over—inch by inch. She had been lightened of every ounce of excess weight. The control cables had been inspected. The motors had been tightened and tuned.

Under Byrd's direction a shovel platoon dug a runway in

front of the great plane. With Balchen at the controls, and with just the nose motor turning, she hauled herself up out of the pit where she had been buried all winter.

Before the base-laying flight could be attempted, a long-planned series of tests had to be made. A number of short flights were made with loads up to 13,000 pounds and up to altitudes of 14,000 feet. Snowblocks, which could be dumped before landing, were used for the weights. Performance was carefully noted under all conditions and from this data it was possible to calculate fuel requirements and to determine how much gasoline would have to be cached at the halfway mark on the Barrier.

On the 18th of November, Bill Haines, the meteorologist, reported to Byrd: "A perfect day. You might have to wait another year for a better one."

With Byrd in command, and doing the navigating, Dean Smith at the controls, Harold June as radioman and relief pilot, and McKinley on the mapping camera, the big plane lifted into the air.

The flight was made without incident to the foot of the glaciers at the base of the Queen Maud Mountains. The fliers followed the trail of the geological party, which was also headed due south. Now and again Byrd checked the ground party's position with his navigating instruments. The trail was true as the flight of an arrow.

Over the roar of the motors, Byrd shouted, "We should pick up the geological party any minute."

McKinley pointed downward. There they were—five teams, struggling in the bitter cold and heavy snow. The men were lashed to the sleds with their dogs, pulling like beasts of burden as they toiled over the surface.

As the plane thundered overhead, white faces turned upward in greeting. Byrd dropped them a bag of miscellaneous equipment which they had requested. Soon the laboring teams were lost in the whiteness.

Now there was no trail to follow. Byrd's navigation had to be absolutely exact. They must know precisely where they were at all times.

Gradually the vast bulk of the mountains rose through the whirling haze of the propellers. They were black, forbidding, capped with snow and slashed with great canyons. Between the peaks poured the ponderous flow of the living glaciers from the Polar Plateau behind. All this had been seen by Amundsen in 1912, and described by him. His charts and descriptions lay on the navigation table before Byrd.

According to Amundsen, there were two gigantic glaciers—he had named them the Axel Heiberg Glacier and the Liv Glacier—over which a pass might be found to reach the plateau beyond. One of these glaciers would have to be selected as a landmark. They would try to land at its base and set up the supply dump.

Anxiously, Byrd and Dean Smith studied the surface below. "What do you think, Dean?" shouted Byrd.

Smith shook his head negatively. Axel Heiberg was out of the question. The whole area below it was a vast field of jumbled drift and enormous crevasses. A landing would be impossible. Byrd motioned him to continue on toward the bulk of Liv Glacier. Perhaps the surface here would be more hospitable.

Everywhere the surface of the Barrier at the foot of the glacier was scored with crevasses and wavelike formations of sastrugi—high drifts resembling sand-dunes, caused by the wind.

Smith pointed farther westward. There lay what seemed to be a patch of fairly level snow, and here they decided to try the landing.

"Drop a smoke bomb, Dick," shouted Dean Smith.

Byrd let the smoke bomb go; its column leaned easily on the wind in an easterly direction. Then he let four go in a line as a help in determining their height above the surface.

As the plane swung in a big circle, engines throbbing, into the wind, Dean Smith looked up at Byrd.

Byrd grinned. "She's all yours, Dean."

Everything now depended on the pilot. He must make a safe landing with an unwieldy, heavy plane, on an unknown terrain. The success of the entire expedition rested on his shoulders. If they cracked up, not only would their lives be endangered and the Polar flight cancelled, but the geological party would have to be diverted from its objectives to render them help.

Again Byrd demonstrated his great faith in other men and his willingness to stand by his evaluation of them. Although a superb flyer himself, he felt in his heart that Smith was the more skillful. Into Smith's hands he entrusted the entire fate of the expedition.

Just before the skis touched, Smith nosed the big metal plane up into a power stall. It hit the snow at about 50 miles an hour. The touchdown was rough—very rough, but the Ford held together, and soon coasted to a stop. Once more they were saved by foresight—in this case Byrd's insistence that the skis be wider and longer than those ordinarily used for snow landings. Had the skis been narrower, or shorter, they might easily have slashed and dug deep into the sastrugi and ended all their hopes in a fraction of a second.

Smith remained in the plane nursing the engines—he did not dare stop them. The others tumbled out, stacking supplies and tins of precious gasoline as fast as they could.

When the work was finished, Byrd called to Smith to pass down his sextant and sun compass. This was one spot whose location must be established without any doubt!

This accomplished, Byrd, McKinley, and June paused a moment to enjoy the view of the enormous Barrier—stretching away, rolling in undulating troughs and crests clear to the horizon to the north. To the south—as yet untraversed—the mighty mountains reared to the sky. Down them poured in stately ponderous masses, the ice of the glaciers. Moving perhaps a foot or two a day, the solid ice behaved exactly like water, forming falls, whirlpools, and eddies under the relentless pressures pushing from behind.

The men were aroused from their reverie by the gunning of the motors. Dean Smith slid a window back from the cockpit.

"Let's get out of here," he yelled. Dean was worried about fuel consumption.

The men hustled back aboard, and a moment later the plane bumped its way over the surface into the air and swung into a long, climbing turn. They headed north, for Little America.

The trip back was hazardous. A leak in a coupling on a main gas line caused them to lose hundreds of gallons of fuel. The motors sputtered to a stop, and again they had to endure the anguish and uncertainty of a landing on the unknown terrain of the Barrier—and this time with a dead stick.

Dean Smith made the touchdown safely, however, no small feat in such a plane. The Ford tri-motors were sluggish, touchy planes. Without power, real skill was needed to manage them.

Since the position of the plane was known at all times to those back in Little America, the small Fairchild under the capable hands of Bernt Balchen was able to make the flight to them with additional gasoline. The repairs in the line were made; the take-off and return to Little America were accomplished without further trouble.

Weather at Little America continued calm—light winds and clear greenish-blue skies. But Byrd delayed the flight to the Pole for two reasons. The mechanics needed time to go over the plane again with a fine-tooth comb. And lastly, he was waiting until Larry Gould and his geological party were in position in the Queen Maud Mountains and could relay weather reports by radio. It might be calm at Little America, while a blizzard raged 300 miles to the south. These weather reports from the half-way point were vital.

"Patience, patience, and still more patience," was Byrd's counsel to his eager crews.

CHAPTER 5

FLYING OVER
THE SOUTH POLE

ON NOVEMBER 28TH, LARRY GOULD AT THE FOOT OF THE Queen Maud Mountains, sent a final weather report. "Weather unchanged. Perfect visibility. No clouds anywhere."

Bill Haines and his staff made their final balloon tests at Little America, consulted their charts for the last time.

The verdict: Now or never. "If you don't go now you may never have another chance as good as this." Haines' face was serious as he made his report to Byrd.

The plane stood poised and set for the take-off. Never had a ship been tuned more carefully.

Byrd nodded briefly, smiled at his crew. "Let's go," he said.

There was a last minute flurry of loading certain pieces of delicate equipment— watches, chronometers, sextants. There were murmurs of "good-bye . . . good luck." The door of the plane slammed shut.

Balchen's steady hands fed gas to the roaring motors, and after a 30-second run, the skis in a great shower of snow lifted clear of the runway at Little America.

The huge wing creaked and groaned in protest as it hoisted the burden of 15,000 pounds into the sky. Then it turned obediently in perfect response to the man at the controls, swung southward and buckled down to the long task ahead.

Byrd gazed downward from the window. He caught a flashing glimpse of the tiny city which represented so much to him—so many hopes, so many dreams.

There was not much to see. Man's puny marks were dwarfed against the immense white stage of the Antarctic. The thin radio towers, a few humps where drift snow had piled over the low rooftops, a few black stove-pipes against the gleaming snow—this was all, except for a handful of men, fur clad and dark against the glitter, waving good-bye.

Today it is difficult to imagine the very real dangers of such a flight. It is hard to realize how much cool courage and determination were required of this handful of men as they took off in their lumbering plane into the Antarctic sky.

In 1928 aviation was barely out of its infancy. Motors were not as reliable as they are now. A speck of dirt in a carburetor could send men plunging to death. Little was known about metals—a weakened strut, a crystallized tiny spring, a cracked piston—any one of a thousand things could spell doom.

The performance capabilities of the three-engined plane were little known. Navigational aids were rudimentary compared to those available to the modern flyer. Byrd himself, with his quick intuitive mind, his thorough background and training and his knowledge of the heavens, was their navigational aid! Except for instruments such as the bubble sextant and the drift indicator, which he himself had designed, the equipment on the *Floyd Bennett* was little more refined than the equipment that had been used by navigators on ships for centuries.

Should the straining motors fail them, should anything happen to disturb the delicate balance between the wallowing plane and the pull of gravity, they would fall like stone to the ice below. With nothing remotely resembling a rescue helicopter, they would be entirely dependent upon their own resources and what aid their comrades with dog teams hundreds of miles away could offer.

From the air, the endless plain of the Barrier looked smooth and beautiful, offering a perfect landing field at any spot. But experience warned them that the appearance was deceptive. Innocent dark lines, networks fanning and leading in all directions told of crevasses, some of them open, some of them bridged by a thin glittering topping of ice. What seemed a smooth rolling field was actually wicked sastrugi, long undulating waves of drift hardened and made gritty by cold—as dangerous to the skis of a plane as the waves of the sea or the dunes of a vast expanse of desert.

Slowly gaining altitude, the plane followed the thin line of tracks which the geological party had made as it sledged south. Sometimes the line did not go straight; it took long detours around belts of crevasses or dangerous sink-holes. By flying a bee-line as calculated from the compass, the plane always picked up the tracks again when they return to their true course.

Throughout the flight Byrd bent over the tiny chart table, taking occasional sights on the sun or lining up the sun compass, figuring, calculating endlessly. He was so busy with his navigation that there was no time for sightseeing! There must be no mistake in his figures now. A slight error, a course which puts them off several miles could mean a half-hour loss of time. And time? Time was gasoline. And gasoline was safety . . . life itself.

He scarcely left the table except to take a sight. Changes in course, comments, instructions, were sent forward to the pilot in the cockpit on a little overhead trolley which the mechanics had rigged.

Except when sending important messages back to Little America, the transmitting key of the ship's radio was tied down. This meant that the transmitter was broadcasting a continuous signal—more than reassuring to their comrades back at the base. As long as the plane's engines were turning, the generators would be feeding the transmitter. As long as those who were waiting heard this steady whine, they knew the plane was in the air, and safe.

Harold June, the radio operator and copilot, was as busy as Byrd himself. Now and again he relieved Balchen at the controls or helped him keep the trail below them in view. He operated the motion picture camera, and most important of all, dumped gasoline from the loose spare cans in the cabin into the main tank. The emptied tins, which weighed two pounds each, were jettisoned out the trap door.

The steady click-click of the big aerial surveying camera never stopped as McKinley shot roll after roll of pictures.

These pictures, which were shot at a known oblique angle toward the horizon, provided the first record ever made of the contours of the Antarctic below them.

Up forward, behind the big nose engine, it was warm. The rest of the cabin was icy cold, and the men were glad to be wearing their fur parkas.

By 8:15 o'clock, about five hours after the takeoff, they saw the geological party camping at the base of the Queen Maud Mountains.

Byrd ordered a letdown, and Balchen dropped the ship to an altitude of about 750 feet. McKinley put overboard some photographs of the Queen Mauds and some other items they had promised to bring. The parachute fluttered open and swung gently back and forth as the load dropped to the snow. Two of the forms clustered about the dark tents detached themselves and ran out to catch it.

In a moment, with a wave and a thumbs-up for luck, the camp was gone. Nothing, no living thing now remained between the plane and the South Pole. The crew girded for the real battle of the flight, a battle filled with unknowns—the struggle to get up over the sawtooth mountains and gaping chasms onto the Plateau itself.

The engines had been running at cruising speed to conserve gasoline. But now altitude was needed.

Byrd signaled Balchen to "wind 'em up." The big Norwegian's steady hands went out to the throttles, advanced them to maximum power. The roar of the engines and propellers deepened. The plane seemed to take a great breath, stretch out, flatten, dig in.

Near the navigating table were two additional altimeters. Byrd watched them as the needles moved in little jumps across the dials—3,000 feet, 4,000, 5,000. The plane had the bit in her teeth now and was climbing fast.

One vital decision still had to be made. Once decided, the consequences would crowd hard on them in seconds. Byrd had to be right.

Ahead lay the peaks of the mountains, black, snowpocked, rearing up out of the glistening whiteness like dark thunder-heads. This is the "hump" over which they must fly. Between the peaks were yawning chasms—the passes. Each chasm was filled with the slow-moving torrent of a living glacier. There were two principal choices—Axel Heiberg and Liv Glacier. Over which would they make their attempt?"

Once committed, there was no retreat, no room to turn and go back. The passes were too narrow.

Anxiously Byrd made his way forward to stand behind Balchen. Together they scanned the glittering waterfalls of ice. Behind them McKinley nonchalantly attended to his work; the click-click of the camera never ceased. June dumped the last of the spare fuel in the tank and threw the cans overboard.

The only thing Byrd really knew about either of these glaciers which lay before them was that Amundsen had reported the crest of Axel Heiberg to be at an altitude of 10,500 feet. Pitifully scant information. This height was perilously close to the maximum ceiling they could hope to get out of the plane, loaded as she was.

His glance turned toward Liv glacier. The crest seemed about the same height, but the pass . . . perhaps it was slightly wider. In a pinch, this extra width might give them the added maneuverability which would mean the difference between life and death.

There was no time to lose. The decision must be made. Now!

Byrd pointed, signaled to Balchen. Liv it would be!

Balchen's grip tightened on the wheel, his jaw hardened. The plane swung and banked hard to the south. This was it!

The floor of the glacier rose steadily beneath them in a stupendous series of ice falls and terraces. Some of the terraces were more than 400 feet above the present height of the climbing plane. The beauty of the graceful swirls and falls of the ice belied the steely hardness and the finality with which it would dispose of the fragile plane, should it fall.

Further along, ten miles up the pass, the ice was cut into gigantic crevasses where it had ground against the rock beneath. Any one of these crevasses could have swallowed a dozen Floyd Bennetts.

The altimeters now showed an altitude of 9,600 feet, and still the slowly flowing river of ice rose in front of the plane. A solid stream of icy air poured out of the plateau, through the top of the crest, and volleyed down the surface of the glacier. The plane leaped and jumped in long swooping, spine-jarring rolls.

Balchen strained to control the ship. There were no auxiliary boosters on the controls of these old ships. Muscle, and muscle alone, did the trick. The veins stood out on his neck and forehead and his hands showed white as they gripped the control pedestal. The ship was fast reaching her ceiling; each moment she became more and more difficult to handle, more and more sluggish, nearing the point where she would fall off in a fatal stall.

Still Balchen kept her at it. Nose up, tail down. She was practically mushing through the air without gaining an inch of altitude.

Byrd braced himself behind the pilot, staring through the spinning haze of the center propeller arc. Vast mountains and ice were on each side, and dead ahead in the center of the summit of the glacier rose a black spire of a rock. It was an awesome sight. This spire of rock rose and fell agonizingly above and below the nose of the ship as Balchen desperately tried to maintain flying speed and at the same time, force the ship to climb.

Balchen took his glance for a second from the job, looked at Byrd. He said nothing, but his meaning was all too clear. They had reached the limit and still needed more altitude. Ahead of them, and above them, the rock approached.

Above the roar of the engines Balchen now yelled, pointed frantically. "Overboard! Overboard! . . . 250 pounds!"

And so another decision was forced on the slender man standing behind him. What would go overboard—food or gasoline?

If gasoline, they might as well try to turn back right now. If food, they would perish in the event of a forced landing.

Anticipating the command, Harold June had moved the big gasoline tank and stood waiting, his hand on the dump valve. McKinley, leaving his camera for a moment, had hauled a bag of their precious emergency food to the trap door. He too awaited the decision.

It came quickly. Byrd signaled to McKinley. "One bag overboard," he shouted above the roar of the engines. In a second the brown canvas bag was gone, spinning down toward the glacier. Fascinated, almost in awe, Byrd and the others watched it burst open on the ice—the precious food gone forever.

The improvement in the plane was instantaneous. She seemed to leap, to dig her toes in for the final climb.

But now, the wind pouring through the crest down the glacier increased. They were so close they could actually see the Polar Plateau ahead and slightly above them. Again, Balchen fought to control the plane, to force it to climb, and at the same time to retain maneuverability. Once again the battle was lost and again, all eyes looked at Byrd.

Food or gasoline?

"Quick, quick!" shouted Balchen. The dark pinnacle of rock swept at them like a nightmare.

And again, food. The last bag. Two hundred and fifty pounds of food, enough for four men for a month, lay scattered on the frigid waste.

The die was cast now, and as though realizing it, the plane clawed at the air for support, leaped forward, lurched higher and higher, straining for altitude. In a moment it was over. The summit and the clutching rock in its center slid beneath the wings.

Balchen leveled off over the Polar Plateau at an altitude of 11,000 feet. Riding the thin tightrope of the racking engines, they soared toward the South Pole. An instant's falter in the steady drum of the motors would send them to crashing death, without food, without possibility of help, lost in an immense continent still in the full grip of the Ice Age.

But the engines did not fail. On and on they throbbed, pulling to the very limits of their capacity.

There was no trail to follow now; this was pure navigation. Byrd scarcely had time to lift his head from his charts. Steadily McKinley snapped his pictures. Occasionally June relieved the exhausted Balchen at the controls.

At last they made a vast circle over the wasteland. According to Byrd's calculations they were over the Pole—over the southern axis of the earth. He checked and rechecked his figures.

Squarely over the Pole he dropped an American flag which was weighted with a stone from the grave of Floyd Bennett. Byrd and Bennett together had dreamt this dream of the long journey—if not in body, then in spirit.

They turned now, and raced for home. Again, it was a problem for the navigator. The gasoline cache had to be hit right on the nose. On the return, Byrd decided to slide down the slope of Axel Heiberg glacier so as to give McKinley a chance to photograph new territory. Soon the pass and the glacier hove into view ahead of the nose of the plane and they began the long, sloping descent down the icy flanks of the glacier.

After a few circling turns, the gasoline cache was located. Because June had made this landing before on the base-laying flight, Byrd signaled him to take the controls. They edged over to Liv glacier, and June brought the ship down smoothly. An hour and fifteen minutes later, with plenty of gas to get them back to Little America, the *Floyd Bennett* rose once more into the air.

Byrd made no attempt to steer a path home by following the old dog trail. They made a bee-line by sun compass, sextant, and drift indicator. A few hours later the ship made a perfect landing at Little America. They were greeted by the men who had stayed at home and had sweated out the trip.

Once again a dream had been realized for Richard Byrd; once again he had prepared, planned, and hoped. Once more he had assaulted the unknown. His restless heart was for the moment at ease.

That night before turning in Byrd sat down at his journal. What to say? Surely such a momentous flight, such a valiant deed was deserving of great words. His head buzzed with weariness as he sought to express what he felt. At last his pen slowly began to move. What did he speak of? The flight? Himself?

"Well, it's done. We have seen the Pole. McKinley, Balchen and June have delivered the goods. If I had searched the world I doubt if I could have found a better team. Theirs was the actual doing. But there is not a man in this camp who did not assist in the preparations for the flight. Whatever merit accrues to the accomplishment must be shared with them."

CHAPTER 6

ROUNDING OUT
THE EXPEDITION

THERE WAS STILL MUCH WORK TO BE DONE DURING THE summer which remained before the return of the ships.

The dramatic flight over the Pole made everything else seem almost anticlimactic, but Byrd drove ahead vigorously to round out the work of the expedition.

A party was dispatched to make an accurate ground survey of the Bay of Whales. A vast aerial survey of the areas to the east of Little America was undertaken. A series of very long flights in the *Floyd Bennett* was made, and much new land was discovered. Byrd named this land after his wife: Marie Byrd Land.

A point which had been the subject of controversy among geographers for years was also tackled. Antarctica is a continent of many mysteries, not the least of which is its exact identity. Many geologists and geographers had contended that the continent was not one continent at all, but rather two vast pieces of land separated by a deep ocean channel which was covered and hidden by ice and snow. Some believed that Antarctica was nothing more than a large group of islands, extending their mountainous tops out of the sea and the ice cap. There was much to support each of these theories.

Byrd's flights tended to prove that the Antarctic is one great solid land mass and that the peaks which thrust up through the glaciers are not island-tops at all, but are rather the tops of stupendous mountain ranges on the continent itself.

December passed in a round of work and productive activity, but as the first weeks of January wore away, an uneasy restlessness pervaded the camp. Byrd was deeply worried, more so than at any other time during the entire trip. The ice pack had not yet broken up. The possibility was very real that the expedition would not be able to get out at all and would have to face another winter on the Barrier.

This would have been possible. With his usual foresight, Byrd had contemplated this eventuality, and emergency rations and fuel had been provided. Not in abundance, but enough to see them through. If at all possible, however, another winter was to be avoided.

The work of the expedition was accomplished. All objectives had been achieved. A number of men in the camp were ill. High time to be going home!

As the ice pack showed no signs of breaking up, and as the approaching winter bared its claws, the situation became desperate. Byrd made arrangements, not very satisfactory to be sure, and very expensive, for him and his men to be taken off by vessels of the whaling fleet if it became necessary. The fleet was about its summer business in the Ross Sea. The masters and owners of these great ships promised to do what they could, but they were not at all encouraging. Only two of the ships managed to penetrate the ice pack, and they already were on their way out. Hunting had not been good, and they themselves had no wish to be frozen in for the winter.

Meantime, the geological party was racing home. On January 19th they arrived and were given a tremendous welcome. These men were green when they started out, but after 1,500 miles of heavy sledging, they arrived home seasoned veterans, their mission accomplished.

Early in February, Little America was informed by radio that the faithful *Eleanor Bolling* and the *City of New York* were prowling along the northern edge of the ice pack. The previous year, when the base was established, the *City* was through the pack and was approaching the Barrier by the end of December.

Plans had to be made to cover all eventualities. McKinley was put in general charge of demobilizing Little America, and the work started. All equipment was graded A, B, C, or D.

Class A included scientific records, a few highly valuable pieces of equipment, and personal gear. In case of a lightning jump, only Class A material would be taken.

Classes B and C were composed of progressively lower ratings of material. Class D included the two airplanes, which could only be taken in the event both ships got through and there was plenty of time.

Soon dog teams were hard at work hauling the equipment

up close to the edge of the Barrier. There, carefully stacked according to priority, it would be loaded on the ships in strict conformity to the time available. For if one of the ships got through, there would scarcely be time to load the men and necessary equipment, before the cold temperatures forced her out again.

Now fell a final cruel blow. It seemed as though the Antarctic, in bitter final anger at these men who had defied it for so many months, was venting all its fury and bending every effort to thwart them. Due to the terrible storms outside the ice pack, the *Bolling* and the *City of New York* began to run short of coal. The *Bolling* transferred all she could spare to the gallant windjammer and started back to New Zealand. Captain Melville, in the *City* continued probing the pack.

Now, whatever happened, the planes could never be removed. Great blocks of snow were piled on the skis which had first been frozen with water in the ice. Wings were lashed and given a negative angle of attack. Thus staked out, they had a fair chance for survival.

A further serious problem arose. One of the radio operators became acutely ill with appendicitis. This meant a decision in a realm about which Byrd knew little.

An operation in the primitive underground tunnels of Little America would be hazardous in the extreme. And even if the operation were successful, the patient in all likelihood could not be moved when a ship did get through the pack. After many conferences with Byrd, Dr. Coman decided to put off the operation, keeping his seriously ill patient as comfortable as possible in the meantime. If the sick man could leave with the ship, he could be transferred to one of the whalers, which carried complete hospital and medical facilities. Meanwhile, plans had to be made for some men to remain behind and care for him if the operation had to be performed at Little America and he was in no condition to be moved to the ship.

One morning a group of men, headed by Dr. Gould, approached Byrd. "Dick," said Larry Gould, "There are ten of us here who request permission to remain another winter at the base."

Byrd was astounded. "Why?"

"There is still much scientific work to be done. Siple is just getting his teeth in his biological studies. Frank Davis feels that he is getting the technique of photographing magnetic variations down pat and another year would provide tremendously valuable data. And I—"

Larry laughed. "You know I'm a geologist before anything else. To complete my records I need time to go to the mountains to the east."

Byrd looked at these men—loyal comrades, all of them. These were men to whom the demands of science were not demands at all, but rather joyous opportunities to work and further man's knowledge. His heart filled with gratitude. Such work would undoubtedly increase enormously the value of the expedition. Then another thought struck him.

"You wouldn't be thinking of Mason, would you?" Mason was the radio man with appendicitis.

Gould's face was expressionless. "If he is unable to be moved, this just might fit in with our plans," he said smoothly.

Byrd's mind raced. He was deeply touched. Finally he smiled

and said gently, "Negative, Larry. If Mason can't be moved, I promise you can stay. But in the meantime I shall do all in my power to get you off. Suppose next year's ice is as bad as this?" He looked at them affectionately, quizzically. "What then?"

At least one small part of the burden was lifted however. If someone had to remain behind to take care of Mason, there would be no problem deciding who would stay.

Word came at last that the *City of New York* had managed to force the ice pack. A radio message from Captain Melville confirmed what Byrd already knew. In effect, it said, "Be ready. We'll hardly have time to shut down the engines. Winter is here!"

Before she reached the Bay of Whales, the *City* waged a truly desperate battle with the sea—blizzards, ice, snow, and mountainous waves. At one time she nearly foundered under the sheer weight of the ice coating her hull and rigging. Along her sides, she carried an ice plate over two feet thick. Captain Melville estimated that she was burdened with over 200 tons of ice—and this on a 500-ton vessel!

But at last she was in—on February 18. She was bruised, battered, splintered, bearing everywhere the evidence of her terrible struggle. Men, equipment, and dogs came tumbling aboard. Everyone camped near the Barrier and helped with the loading. Everyone, that is, but Dr. Coman and his patient, who remained behind till the last in the ghostly, deserted tunnels of Little America. The man's condition was really serious, and the Doctor decided not to move him until the very final moment.

Early the next morning, Mason was strapped on a sledge.

The dogs quickly made the run to the Barrier's edge, and he was hoisted aboard.

Only Balchen and Byrd remained at Little America. Their last act was to lower Old Glory, tattered and shredded but still streaming in the freezing wind.

Quickly they skied down to the Barrier and climbed aboard the *City*. At 9:30 Captain Melville gave the order to cast off.

A little group of men gathered on the stern of the ship as she crept through the already forming pancake ice toward the pack. Behind her, black and cold, swirled the clouds of sea smoke—final, indisputable harbinger of winter. Like a derisive flag it whirled about them—a flag flown at the men who had dared the continent's fury to gaze upon her jealously guarded secrets. In the face of what was still unknown, they had learned little. But it was more than the Antarctic had ever yielded before, and upon it greater knowledge for mankind would be built.

Some of the men looked back with relief, some with hatred; some with respect. Some regarded the white mistress of the Antarctic as a loathsome devil, others as a vast storehouse of as yet unrevealed knowledge. Others looked on the continent as an implacable enemy, and still others, who would willingly have stayed another year, as a fascinating friend. All, however, were joyful to be going home.

What about Richard Byrd? What was the Antarctic to him? A friend, an enemy, a storehouse of knowledge, a hate-filled beast, a beautiful maiden—all these, yes. But above all, here was a place where a man could find out what he was. Where he could find out what he amounted to.

The goddess of the Antarctic was like the Lorelei, those beautiful, legendary maidens who irresistibly lured men to their destruction, but who sang so sweetly that once their song was heard, there was no forgetting it.

The song of adventure, of excitement. The song of matching one's heart and spirit with the unknown. The song whose words reached clear into a man's spirit and spoke of what it found there. Long ago Byrd had heard this song. When he was 13 and on his way around the world alone. Flying over the North Pole. Flying across the Atlantic. Battling up the windy canyons of Liv glacier. Byrd had heard the song. The siren song. He would be back.

Byrd turned to the parka-clad man standing beside him. "We'll be back," he said.

Bill Haines grinned wryly. "Not me, Dick. Once is enough."

"We'll be back, Bill," said Byrd quietly.

Haines looked at his leader curiously, then he turned without out a word and went below to read his mail.

Byrd stared a moment longer into the swirling drift of the rising storm. He sucked the rich, pure air of the Antarctic deep into his lungs, then he, too, turned and went below.

CHAPTER 7

NEW PLANS

THE SOUTH NEVER CEASED TO CALL HIM BACK. Like beckoning sprites dancing elusively through the sea smoke and blizzard drift they called. Byrd looked and listened and answered the call.

No sooner was the first expedition demobilized than he was hard at the task of forging a second.

Many people thought that Byrd's expeditions were financed by the government. Others believed that he was a wealthy man, or that he was provided with unlimited funds by a great corporation or by a society interested in geographical exploration.

Nothing could be farther from the truth. He raised all the money himself, by hard work, and assumed entire responsibility for it. Often he drove himself, his family, and the entire expedition perilously close to bankruptcy.

Money came in from various sources. He earned a great deal by writing and lecturing about his trips. The rest he begged, or borrowed. Individuals, rich and poor, contributed according to their means and their interest in his undertakings.

His expeditions departed, leaving behind them a great stack of deferred bills and promissory notes, all of which he must pay by money earned from personal appearances, radio broadcasts, books, magazine articles, and the like. In addition to directing the activities of an expedition, then, Byrd had on his mind constantly the agony of this mountain of debt facing him when he returned home.

This meant, among many other things, that his expeditions had to be successful. Who would pay money to read or hear about an Antarctic party which had met with disaster, or which had failed in some glaring way to accomplish what it had set out to do?

Preliminary work for the second Antarctic expedition was finished. The list of all the requirements was drawn up. It is hard to imagine the enormous number of things which were necessary to maintain a company of men in a place which furnished them with nothing but the air they breathed, and a little seal meat! Nuts, bolts, canvas, cloth, needles, thread, sewing machines, pemmican for men and pemmican for dogs, dehydrated vegetables, rope, knives, matches, pots, pans, overalls were only a part of the supplies required.

The final calculations were made. The Navy lent Byrd an old empty warehouse in Boston, and he set to fill it up!

Byrd once said that the dangers of exploring—gales, crevasses, ice, snow, hunger—are nothing compared to the financial storms which the explorer must weather before he even arrives in the field!

The second Antarctic expedition was planned to cost about $500,000. Of this sum, by straining every facility of his own and by begging from every person who would listen, Byrd was able to raise about $150,000. In his efforts he encountered not only indifference and opposition, but sometimes actual resentment. This was in 1931 and 1932, when the United States was deep in the grip of one of the blackest business depressions in our history. Why spend money in the frozen Antarctic when people were out of jobs at home?

He had $150,000. What about the rest? First of all, many of the items did not have to be bought. Various manufacturing companies and societies were willing to donate materials, even if they wouldn't, or couldn't, give money. Oil companies, meat-packing corporations, firms constructing radio equipment, photography equipment, shoes, clothing, coal—as time went on a great many chipped in to help. Slowly the supplies began to pile up in the old warehouse.

Still there was never enough! As Byrd humorously put it, every explorer since Columbus has finally had to work on a percentage basis—that is, somebody puts up the money and the explorer gives them the right to share in the loot! The trouble with Polar exploration though, is that there isn't any loot. No gold, no silver, no diamonds. Maybe a donor could have a mountain named after him in return for his cash, but that was about all. Beyond this, there is nothing to show for such an expedition except maps of useless, frozen lands and a great mass of scientific data which might not have any real value for years to come.

But there was a way for Byrd to get around this. Endorsements! In return for the right to advertise their products as being used under rigorous Polar conditions, many more companies contributed necessary supplies.

There were, of course, many things that could not be donated. Hard cash was still necessary. The $150,000 seemed mighty small, and was going fast. The men on the expedition were volunteers and most of them received no pay at all; however, money had to be put aside to take care of their families while they were gone. Many articles of equipment were not donated and had to be bought. Laborers and artisans who did the overhauling of the ships had to be paid. The list seemed endless; soon the supply of cash was gone and Byrd commenced the borrowing! His only security was his own good name and promises to write books, to speak over the radio, to write newspaper and magazine articles. All hope of payment lay in the future, and all was without any value whatsoever if the expedition were a failure.

Gradually, the expedition took shape. The word was going around—Byrd would sail again for the Antarctic in the fall of 1933! And the men— the men, too, were starting to shake down, be selected for the trip. Thousands applied and out of them all, Byrd had somehow to choose the handful who seemed most capable.

Most warming of all to the harassed man who directed and planned and hoped and dreamed, the old timers began drifting back to him. From all over the world they came—the veterans, among whom he could form a nucleus and around whom the newcomers could be molded and shaped into effective members of the expedition. They drifted in one by one, by twos, by threes. Harold June, the copilot over the South Pole; Bill Haines, the meteorologist who had said that "once was enough," and many others. All told, out of the 42 men who had gone through the first winter in Little America, 18 showed up to make the trip again, completely unable, like Byrd, to resist the lure of the Antarctic! More than anything else, the fact that these men were willing once again to entrust their lives to Byrd is a permanent, lasting tribute to his qualities as a leader.

Two ships had been obtained. The first, a United States Shipping Board "three-island" freighter christened the *Jacob Ruppert*, was leased from the Government for one dollar. She was a steel vessel, like the *Bolling*, and could not be expected to work in pack ice.

The staunch old *City of New York* had literally been worn out on the first expedition and would be of no further use. She was ending her days ingloriously as a kind of floating museum, towed from port to port. However, a rugged wooden ice ship, a veteran of the Alaska trade, lay in the yards in Oakland, California. She was just what Byrd wanted—equipped with sails, with auxiliary power and very heavily built. Christened the *Bear of Oakland*, she was sailed through the Panama Canal to New York for the final outfitting and strengthening.

And still the struggle for money went on. Right up to the last minute it never ceased to plague Byrd. Some of the stratagems which he had to use would have been downright comical had it not been for the desperate need which made them necessary. For example, the *Jacob Ruppert* needed four thousand tons of ballast to weigh her down so the propeller would be deep under the water while working near ice. This much pig iron would cost $50,000! Even rock and sand, counting hauling charges, were too expensive. Finally, Byrd called the president of a large coal company. Would the man "lend" him several thousand tons of coal for two years? Byrd promised to pay for it, if through any accident, he was unable to return it. Meantime, the coal company would have free storage, and possibly, if the price went up during this time, a greater profit two years hence. The man took a gambler's chance and the *Ruppert* was ballasted.

Byrd was more convinced than ever that one of the secrets of successful Antarctic exploration was mechanization. Four planes were obtained—one of them a large Condor biplane, with an enormous lifting capacity. In addition, the party was equipped with snowmobiles for short hauls, and with three heavy-duty crawler-type tractors able to haul enormous weights.

Tractors and planes were important aids, but at this time they had yet to prove their worth in snow, ice, and subfreezing temperatures. No one knew how they would perform over long periods of time in such extremely rigorous conditions. Byrd knew that the absolutely reliable means of transportation in Polar regions was the Husky. Accordingly, on this expedition, as on the former, he saw to it that there were plenty of dogs in the company. When the expedition finally sailed for the South there were 153 powerful sledge dogs with them—mostly from the North—Canada, Alaska, and Labrador. They were of all breeds and sizes, but they all had one thing in common: a love for hard work on the ice.

The objectives of this second expedition included no such spectacular, public-fancy catching feats as the flight over the South Pole.

As Byrd suggested, geographical exploration is, of course, the "brightest weapon in the explorer's armory . . . but it is principally a tool for getting at something deeper. It attains the dignity of a science only when, rising above the superficial glory of the first penetration, it brings the apparatus of science to bear upon the *unknown* . . . for a truer understanding of many problems."

Byrd's first expedition had yielded enormously, had contributed greatly to breaking down the walls of ignorance which surrounded the continent of Antarctica. But it was only a pinprick. Byrd's efforts were hardly a breach, a toe-hold, in this enormous land.

He was determined that this time the fullest effort would be made to "bring the apparatus of science to bear on the unknown." The expedition would be as strongly staffed as it was humanly possible for it to be, both in equipment and in personnel. They were to investigate geology, glaciology, meteorology, botany, biology, zoology, physics, magnetism, oceanography, and many other subjects. Some 22 divisions of scientific endeavor were to be assaulted.

The expedition planned on several important innovations in their research activities. Cosmic ray investigations of the crystal-clear atmosphere of these southern latitudes promised to yield exciting information. The same was true of meteor observations, to be recorded simultaneously with a world-wide chain of observatories. Seismic experiments, such as are used by oil companies to locate fields of petroleum, were to be made to determine the thickness of the Antarctic ice cap and the contours of the earth beneath it. Nothing was overlooked or left undone that might increase the capabilities of the expedition and so add to the store of knowledge about many natural phenomena.

What of Byrd himself? What ramparts did he personally intend to assault? Was it enough for him merely to be the organizer, the skilled leader of a band of men who were going to bring back highly technical information on a wide variety of subjects, most of which he personally knew very little about? This time there were no spectacular "stunts." No Pole to fly over. Perhaps this time his restless, questing spirit would somehow find a greater challenge.

The Antarctic holds many secrets. Not all of them are locked in its skies, beneath its eternal mantle of ice, or inside its gaunt mountains.

Some of them are locked in the hearts of the men who go there. In this ruthless world nothing remains long hidden, nothing that is sham can long endure. The camouflage which a man erects about himself to hide what is in his heart and his spirit is soon stripped away in the Antarctic. He stands naked and alone, revealing to all his comrades, and most of all to himself, what he really is.

So perhaps some greater quest than the thirst for scientific knowledge drove Richard Byrd south again. Perhaps there were questions about himself, which must be answered to himself, that still remained.

Surely he had been put to the supreme test dozens of times

in his life. Surely he must be satisfied. There was nothing he had to prove—to his own heart nor to any living man. But there was something more, there was something beyond this even. Perhaps his soul was reaching beyond his personal hopes and dreams, was groping into the little known realms of the spirit, desirous of turning, to look itself squarely in the eye and know itself for what it was.

Perhaps there was this final citadel to be conquered—the citadel of Richard Evelyn Byrd.

CHAPTER 8

THE SECOND EXPEDITION

AS THE SUMMER OF 1933, MUGGY AND HOT, WORE TO a close, the multitude of loose ends were gradually being tied in place. Like the last pieces of an enormous, chaotic jigsaw puzzle, the final parts of the picture began to be filled out. This was a time of wild desperation and jumbled confusion. There was too much to be done in all too little time.

To quote from Byrd: ". . . it was all uproar, all uncertainty, a shouting confusion of telephones and telegrams, hammers banging, hand trucks rumbling, orders and counterorders, wild-goose chases. Not until the ships had actually slipped their moorings did I dare admit we were really going. Too many matters hung by a thread almost to the last hour."

It was also a time when men demonstrated faith, loyalty and

unswerving devotion. They worked around the clock, finally dropping from sheer fatigue. Any departure can be a nerve-racking experience, but the departure of a great expedition, outbound into the unknown for two years, is pure agony.

The affection which men held for Byrd was never more fully demonstrated than at this time. One afternoon, for example, he spotted a pair of familiar shoulders deep in Ruppert's hold. He studied them for a moment.

"Dana," he shouted. "Dana Coman."

The sweating man looked up from his hand truck to the main deck. It was indeed Dana Coman, the physician on the first expedition, and now head of a clinic at a famous medical school and hospital in the East.

Byrd scrambled down the steel ladder into the hold and pumped the hand of his old friend.

"Dana," he said," What are you doing here?"

Dr. Conan grinned a bit sheepishly. "Well, Dick." he said, "I can't make it with you this trip, but you don't think I could let you get away without giving you a hand, do you?"

What could Byrd say? He muttered thanks, and turned away to hide the quick emotion which sprang to his face. Dr. Coman knew what a heartbreaking ordeal the last few days in port could be, so he had left his hospital, his clinic, donned a pair of dungarees, and joined the crew to give his old friend a hand.

At last the crates and boxes were stowed, and the last goodbyes said. The engine-room telegraph swung to "Full Ahead" and the *Ruppert* stood out to sea. The endless problems and vexations were behind. Ahead lay many other problems, but somehow, to Byrd, these seemed different. A man could cope with them.

He drew a deep breath of relief. At the head of a well-equipped expedition, stiffened and strengthened by a tough core of hardened veterans, he was supremely confident. Given a little luck, there was nothing that could not be accomplished.

The *Bear* was the slower ship and had already left port. Almost immediately, however, she had bored into a severe hurricane and very nearly foundered. The crew was able to bring her limping back to harbor, but she had been so heavily damaged that dry-docking was necessary.

The *Ruppert* sailed on October 22, and the *Bear* made fit for sea again, left November 1. The two ships were to meet again three months later in rendezvous at the Ross Barrier in the Bay of Whales.

The *Ruppert* carried the big Condor biplane, which for the time being was equipped with pontoons. As the vessel neared Antarctica, the plane was swung out a number of times to make mapping and surveying flights.

At long last, in the middle of January, the *Ruppert* approached Little America.

Byrd, Haines, and several of the other veterans stood on deck looking ashore with deep emotion. Here had been their home for long months. Here they had worked, suffered, been bored, had hoped and dreamed—run through the entire gamut of human experience.

Slowly the *Ruppert* cruised close to the Barrier. At last the telegraph rang from "Dead Slow Ahead" to "Slow Astern," in the long black swells of the Ross Sea.

The motor launch was swung outboard, dropped in the water and rounded the stern of the ship to the gangway.

Byrd's plan, of course, was to re-occupy Little America if possible. The old quarters would serve beautifully as a start and could be enlarged as necessary. Much digging and hard work could be saved if the buildings and tunnels were still intact.

The motor launch made a trip to the Barrier and discharged her passengers, then returned to the *Ruppert* for the dog teams and sledges.

Just as on the previous expedition, the moment the Huskies hit the snow and ice, they went utterly mad. After three and a half months in cages on a steel deck, suffering terribly from the heat of the tropics, they could not find ways enough to express their joy at being back in their natural environment. They howled, barked, yipped. They ate the snow, rolled insanely in it, dashed crazily about in wide circles. In a moment the landing spot was a melee of tangled and broken harness, nearly hysterical dogs, overturned sledges, sweating and swearing drivers.

Bill Haines looked at the hopelessly snarled five-ring circus. He grinned. "Seems like we're home, Dick," he said to Byrd. "A complete mess. Right from the start."

Byrd laughed. "Normal all right, Bill." Then he fell silent, gazing up the long glistening incline which lay ahead of them. Little America should be just beyond the crest, in the slight depression he had chosen nearly five years ago. What would they find?

Now was no time to wait until the dogs were under control. "Let's go," he said.

He, Haines, and a number of others, started up the long slope on foot, sinking to their knees in snow at every step.

At last they topped the ridge. Just as they remembered, but somehow altered and changed, was Little America. As they started down the hill the details of the city became sharper and clearer.

There were the three radio towers, still up, still intact, although one of them was slightly out of line, as though a bit weary holding its own against the gales of the past years. There was a flag marker, still bright orange against the white. A little farther along a broom handle—humble reminder of that simplest and homiest of all tasks, housekeeping—stuck up through the snow. There was the anemometer pole, a good four or five feet above the snow, its cleats a reminder of the many painful times it had been climbed to clear away the ice and rime from its whirling cups.

Little America lay quiet, glistening and clean—waiting for them. Byrd and his veterans surveyed the scene briefly for a moment, then started calling to each other's attention things and places and events long past.

Strangely enough, their memory was not as accurate as they had thought. The old trails and distances—so many steps from the Mess Hall to the Administration Building for example—a figure they had thought would have been etched forever on their minds, escaped them. Other things too, had slipped their memories: the location of tunnels, entry-ways, emergency exits and so on.

At last Bill Haines stopped dead. "Right here," he said. "I know I'm right. Here is my old theodolite station. Straight down."

Byrd handed him a snow shovel. "Go to it," he said.

Haines grunted wryly. "Now I know I'm home," he said.

"When I left here I swore I wouldn't touch one of those things ever again. We haven't been ashore an hour and you stick one in my hands."

Byrd laughed. He and Bill Haines started digging. Three or four feet down, sure enough, the shovels struck the roof of the old observatory. A moment later the trapdoor was off and Haines slipped inside. Byrd could hear him chuckling and laughing from the darkness of the hole below. He slid through after him.

The room was pitch black, but after lighting a match Byrd found a fruit jar half full of kerosene. He put the match to the wick and surprisingly enough, it lit. The shadows jumped back, and as they did, a full tide of memories flooded in. They were joined now by the other members of the party.

Actually, there was very little change. The walls and ceilings were covered with a film of ice, and fantastic stalactites hung from the beams. Some of these beams had been broken and crushed by the weight of the snow, and in other places the walls of the tunnels had collapsed.

The thing which astonished even Byrd was the disorder. Torn parkas and windproofs were scattered about. Underwear, unmatched stockings, worn out boots, and other items of equipment cluttered the floors and bunks. Dirty dishes lay in the sink and half-eaten food was on the table.

Dr. Poulter, the head scientist of the expedition, and soon to be appointed by Byrd as second-in-command, looked at the mess. He grinned and chided, "My but you fellows were untidy housekeepers. The place needs a good cleaning out."

Byrd could only laugh and agree, recalling the haste with

which Little America had been abandoned and its people and gear loaded on the old *City of New York.*

Queer, the memories that all this brought back. For example, there on a dirty and littered table was a loaf of bread, a half-filled coffeepot and a hunk of roast whale meat with a fork still stuck in it. A very sloppy sight, one which no good housewife would go away and leave. But this had been the lunch of the last man to leave the Mess Hall—Dr. Coman, who had stood a lonely vigil by the side of Mason, the radio operator who had been so ill with appendicitis. When word came, they had to leave quickly. Dr. Coman's fork was just where he had left it. The meat and the other food were perfectly preserved after all this time by the intense cold.

As Byrd stood there, reminiscing for a brief moment in the half darkness, a remarkable thing happened . . . the telephone rang!

Byrd picked up the receiver. A faraway voice said: "You left me behind, Dick. Been waiting a long time for you to come back."

Byrd's breath caught in his throat, then his expression turned to laughter as he recognized Dr. Poulter's voice calling from the Administration Building. The batteries which operated the telephone system still worked beautifully, preserved by the cold.

And then, another miracle. Byrd pressed a light switch, and the globes dimly came to life.

Everything worked. Even the food, years old, was completely edible when warmed and thawed. Other stores which they found—canned beans, seal meat, flour—were all preserved.

Little America, with a bit of tidying up, would shelter them all again, and would even contribute to their supplies.

Someone wound the old phonograph. The needle was poised, a record was already in place. The strains of "The Bells of Saint Mary's" pealed through the shacks and tunnels. This broke the party of veterans up, much to the astonishment of the newcomers. How were they to know that this record had been played and played so many times during the previous occupation that it had become a joke. It was almost the National Anthem of Little America.

But the time for memories was past. Work was waiting. Dr. Poulter was put in charge of rehabilitating the city; Byrd returned to the ship.

Now began the "white nightmare" as Byrd called it. The battle to unload. It began on January 18, and the expedition very nearly foundered because of it.

The entire Bay of Whales was choked with pressure ice, just as it had been on the previous expedition. Now, however, the small inlet which they had previously used was also blocked. A belt of jumbled ice about a half-mile wide ran completely along the shoreline. Constantly changing and shifting, it had no stability.

Skiers were dispatched to find a route around this area. They found one, but the distance was over 20 miles between the ship and Little America., although as the gull flies it was scarcely two and a half miles.

The punishment of unloading hundreds and hundreds of tons of supplies and transporting them such a distance was unthinkable. They would still be working when the winter night fell.

The skiers were dispatched again. A way must be found through the pressure ice. They needed a route which would support the weight of dogs and loaded sledges as well as the tractors and their loads.

The choices, as always in the Antarctic, were brutally clear. The long trip around to Little America was impossible. The establishment of a new Little America which would be more accessible would have to be undertaken only as a last resort.

Patiently the skiers and surveyors probed a trail though the tangle of the pressure ice and marked it with orange flags. The two and a half miles from the ship to Little America stretched to seven. Seven man-killing miles. The route was passable, yes, but only slowly and at great sacrifice. Misery Trail, the men called it, and the name was appropriate.

As on the first expedition, the heavily loaded *Jacob Ruppert* was moored next to the Barrier. The men unloaded as fast as possible onto the ice, got the supplies away from the edge, and stacked them near the edge of the pressure belt. Here it was divided into lighter sledge loads and pulled over Misery Trail by the dogs.

Slowly a tiny trickle of equipment started to move into Little America, to be received by Dr. Poulter and a small crew, and stored in the rehabilitated tunnels and houses.

Rush, rush, rush. Time is master in the Antarctic and every man felt the lash of its whip. Day and night. On watch and off. Officers, cooks, scientists, seamen worked at the task.

Men worked past weariness, past knowing, past caring what they were doing. They started on errands; when they arrived at their destination they had forgotten why they had come. The blinding pain of utter fatigue burned and seared—and yet somehow the job went ahead. Over them all whirled the thin yellow Antarctic sun—impersonal and relentless.

The *Bear* arrived with more supplies. She moored alongside the *Ruppert* and the battle of unloading increased in tempo.

To add to the troubles, although in one way it was a blessing, the summer this year was a very long one. This gave the men additional weeks to accomplish their task, but it also meant that the ice began to rot, to soften, to crumble and give way beneath the weight of the sledges.

The equipment was divided into three categories, starting with that which was absolutely essential. Additional caches were made just beyond the pressure ice, half way to Little America.

The *Ruppert* left and finally the *Bear*. The latter ship had to face another round trip to New Zealand. The doctor who had come with the expedition fell ill. Furthermore, the additional gasoline consumption caused by the terrible strain on the tractors had caused the supply to run dangerously short.

The *Bear* returned with more gasoline, and with Dr. Potaka, a friendly, likable young man.

The time was late February, no month for a ship to be caught in the Ross Sea. The *Bear* lost not time in getting away. Byrd and the winter party watched their last link with civilization vanish into the darkness and sea smoke of winter.

The battle to convey all the gear to Little America continued until darkness fell in May. But at least the ships had been unloaded and supplies discharged—even if most of them were still strung out in great depots all along the trail.

There was time now for Byrd to think of other matters. He dispatched a surveying party to pick out and mark a trail for the summer parties which would be organized during the winter. He made a few flights on which a considerable amount of aerial surveying was accomplished.

Beyond this activity, there was little that could be done. The travail of unloading the ships had left enormous damage in its wake. The men were worn out, exhausted. The dogs were down to skin and bones. Some of the tractors had broken down completely; the others were limping badly, desperately in need of repair and thorough overhaul. But there was much to be thankful for.

As the summer drew to a close, and as the huge mountains of supplies were stowed away under the ice at Little America, once more the objectives, the hopes and the dreams of the expedition could be considered.

The dreams—the eternal questings of man. Throughout the dark winter months, throughout the months of sunlight which would follow, what questions would be answered for each of the men at Little America?

What questions about himself, what answers, would Richard Byrd find? What final summits would this quiet man climb?

CHAPTER 9

PROJECT—ADVANCE BASE

MANY MONTHS PRIOR TO THE SAILING OF THE expedition, a skilled cabinet-maker labored long and hard in an obscure loft in Boston. He was building a small shack, although shack is hardly the word to describe such a perfect product of his art. It was more like a perfectly fitted jewel box.

When finished, he stepped back, and looked with pride on his work. Then he picked up the phone and called Byrd.

Byrd came with Paul Siple, a veteran of the first expedition who was also going on this one. The two men looked approvingly at the shack. It embodied every pet idea of design and every safety feature that long experience in the Antarctic had indicated would be necessary and desirable.

The little dwelling was made so that it could be knocked

down and transported easily. The sections were doweled together so perfectly that one could hear the air squishing out when they were put together.

The walls were only four inches thick, but they had been built up of alternating layers of plywood and insulating materials. The inside was covered with a heavy layer of fireproof canvas. A trapdoor was installed in the roof, and the pins which held it were arranged so that it would work either way. If covered too deeply with snow, it could be pulled down, so the men inside could dig their way out.

A heavy door in one wall—something like the door to a walk-in refrigerator, would give the occupants easy access to tunnels which were to be dug in the snow and ice for storage purposes.

A system of pipes for ventilation had been worked out. The circulation of air depended upon the delicate balance between the weight of hot and cold air.

An oil-burning stove of special design for work in temperatures which would drop far, far below zero was also provided. It, of course, had its own special outlet, like a chimney, through the roof.

The shack was designed for three occupants. It was small—only 9 by 13 by 8-feet, but this was more than ample for explorers accustomed to living within arm's reach of each other.

Siple and Byrd examined the shack admiringly. In spite of its numerous innovations, in spite of the fact that it was portable, it was strong and rigid. Like the steel turret of a battleship, it should be more than capable of resisting the strongest winds and blizzards.

Tinglof, the cabinet-maker, had done his work well. Byrd

was more than satisfied. Furthermore, the tiny house would be thoroughly tested at Little America, and if any final changes were to be made, the cabinet-maker would be available. He was going south with them.

The shack was dismantled, crated, and stowed deep in the hold of the *Ruppert*. Not a half-dozen men of the expedition knew what it was for.

Now, many months later, the snug building had been erected right in the middle of Little America. It was the only building that was not sunk beneath the surface of the snow. It stuck out like a sore thumb, high above the barrier surface.

One morning late in March, Byrd walked across the snow to the entrance of the shack.

Around him the hullabaloo of the unloading and the constructing of quarters was in full swing. The crisp air rung to the shouts of the men, the barking of dogs, the "Hi, Hi, Hi" of the drivers, the clatter and roar of tractors, and the hammering of busy carpenters. Preparations for the winter were going ahead full blast.

Byrd opened the door. Inside it was warm and comfortable.

"Good morning, Paul," he said to the tall young man who was bent seriously over the stove. From inside came the friendly hiss of oil burning in the grate.

Byrd looked with surprise at the stove. This was not the special one they had brought down from the States. This was an ordinary black, cast-iron heater. Instead of burning coal, an oil kindler had been fitted.

"What happened to the other stove?" asked Byrd.

Paul Siple shook his head. He had been living in the shack

since its erection on the ice, testing it, considering it from every angle. A shack which worked well in theory and which looked beautifully efficient in a loft in Boston might develop surprising quirks in the Antarctic. These men were too wise and too well aware of the hazards of life on the Barrier to leave anything to chance.

Again, Paul Siple shook his head and sighed wearily. He was pale and tired.

Letting his question go, Byrd looked at Paul carefully. "You are a little green around the gills," he said.

"That's right, Dick. And that's why the stove is changed."

"What happened?"

"Fumes. That patent stove looks great on paper and maybe it would be great in a big room with plenty of ventilation. But not here. It almost got me last night."

Fumes from stoves and heaters were a constant problem in the tight dwellings where the men lived. Carbon monoxide, given off by burning coal and oil, is a deadly poison. Odorless, colorless, it never announces itself. Its victims usually never know they are being poisoned until too late.

"So?" said Byrd, highly interested. "How did it affect you?"

"Dizzy. Nausea. Headache. Caught myself just in time."

"Sure it wasn't something you ate?" asked Byrd. Many of the men were complaining of stomach disorders. Too much fatigue and too little sleep. Food poorly and hastily prepared and literally eaten on the fly had gotten many of them down.

Immediately Byrd regretted asking the question. Paul Siple was no hysterical newcomer. He had been with Byrd as a Boy Scout on the first expedition, and while he was still young in years, he was old in the seriousness of his attitudes and in his ability to reason and think. If Paul said it had been the stove, then it was the stove. No two ways about it.

"I'm sorry, Paul. I should have known better than to ask such a question," apologized Byrd. "How about this one?" He indicated the makeshift heater.

"I don't like it much either," said Paul. "It isn't made for oil in the first place. It just isn't tight enough. In the door or the top." He looked at the stove dubiously.

Byrd walked over to the air inlet pipe which rose through the center of the floor. Standing on a box he held his hand above the opening. A steady stream of cold air was flowing in.

"Plenty of air coming," he commented.

Siple nodded agreement. "Sure. More than enough for three men. But how about bad weather? A week's blizzard at 60 or 70 below?"

"I know," said Byrd. Siple was overlooking nothing. They both knew that under such conditions the ventilating pipe could easily be choked with ice and rime.

He thought a moment.

"Tell you what, Paul," he said. "Let me move into the shack for a few weeks. I'll keep the stove burning day and night. We'll plug the ventilator and see what happens under every conceivable condition."

This was so like Byrd. Siple looked at his leader and laughed. "Trust you, Dick. You wouldn't let anybody go out under circumstances you weren't sure were safe."

"If I feel any ill effects at all, we'll tackle the problem some other way. Make some more changes. If we can't lick it we'll cancel the project. Nothing is worth more than the lives of the men."

"I agree," said Paul Siple. Then he said, curiously, "Who've you picked out to go, Dick?

Byrd smiled. The question came more and more often these days. He felt he could confide in Paul, if anyone, but he himself didn't know. "I don't know yet Paul. Three men—a radio operator, meteorologist, and a mechanic." He laughed. "I don't understand it. Everyone wants to go."

Byrd moved into the shack, made it his headquarters. He and Siple tested the stove and the ventilation in as many ways as they could think of. Everything worked perfectly.

And so the project of Advance Base began to evolve into its final shape.

One of Byrd's greatest interests was meteorology. He wanted to study the great aurora australis which flamed across the dark sky during winter, the fall of meteors, and above all, weather itself. The speed and direction of the wind, barometer readings, humidity readings, temperatures—all of these matters were important and vital.

The big problem, the one which he hoped to lick in part with Advance Base, was that of co-ordinated readings. All his records so far had been taken at one spot. If readings could be synchronized— in other words, if the scientists could know what was happening at two observation points hundreds of miles apart at the same time, the value would be enormous. The mystery of weather would in part be breached. This was his dream for the future—a whole chain of weather stations taking synchronized readings.

But—one thing at a time. The time is now. Now they would get readings from two stations, Little America and Advance Base.

This was the purpose of the shack. It was to be sunk in the ice far to the south, and when manned, would be able throughout the long, lonely winter to record data and radio back vital information to the station at Little America.

Again, it was rush, rush, rush. The demon of time was cracking his whip. Winter was racing across the ice. Already it was too late to think of transporting the shack and supplies to the originally planned location at the foot of the Queen Maude Mountains, 400 miles to the south.

The ghastly battle to unload the ships had used up golden weeks of time. The dogs were worn out, and besides, the pick of the pack had already been sent on a scouting expedition under the command of Captain Innes-Taylor, a veteran driver. This party was returning, but would arrive far too late to be of any use. In addition, even had all the dogs been available, and in the pink of condition, it was doubtful if they could have transported all the supplies necessary.

If Advance Base were to succeed at all, it would have to be transported by the tractor fleet, and here again, was difficulty. The machines had been sorely punished. Some of them had been overhauled, some were being worked on. How many would be ready, and how soon?

Byrd soon realized that Advance Base would have to be a far more modest effort than originally planned.

He called Bill Haines. "Bill," he said, wearily, "I doubt if Advance Base can be pushed to the Queen Maudes. We'll never make 400 miles and back with all the gear. I doubt if we'll make 300 miles—or even 200."

Haines smiled. "What's your most realistic figure, Dick?"

Byrd said, very carefully, observing Haines' reaction, "It all depends. The tractors and sledges are about loaded. They'll start in a few days. How far will they get? Depends on the weather and on how the machines hold up."

"How far do you think?" insisted his old friend.

Byrd looked at Haines narrowly. "We'll hope for 150 miles. Will that do you any good?"

Haines smiled. "I thought you were going to name a lower figure." He, too, knew the difficulties of punching a trail southward and setting up a base this time of year. "I'd give my eye teeth for simultaneous readings between Little America and any spot over a hundred miles out."

Byrd knew that Haines was right. Little America was in a protected basin. Its climate was relatively mild, compared to that of the interior of the Barrier, where the blizzards came shrieking and howling across thousands of miles of ice. He rose, smiled at Haines. "You'll get them Bill. I promise. At least a hundred miles out."

Slowly the pattern of Advance Base evolved, moved inexorably on toward its end.

Byrd watched the caravan of tractors—three of them—a big American machine and two smaller French machines, creep out across the snow to the south, their exhausts pouring and spouting white vapor into the air.

How far would they get? So much depended on this. Although they dragged loaded sledges behind them and were themselves stowed to the brim, they carried only enough supplies for one man throughout the winter. If, as originally planned, three men were to man the station, they must make another trip. Could the worn out tractors and the exhausted men do it? Byrd watched them leave with deep misgivings.

The answer came soon by radio. Impossible crevasses, storms, soft snow. Progress was pitifully slow. The big tractor broke down. The two smaller machines must go on, unload, then return to pick up the material from the cripple. Could they do all this and still have time to make another round trip to Little America?

Obviously not, and the next decision was hard. Three men could not make it. Then how about two? And if not two, could one man survive by himself through the winter? If the answer was yes, who would it be? Byrd pondered long.

Then he called a meeting of picked men—some veterans, some not, but all absolutely reliable.

There were present Dr. Poulter, the senior scientist, a great giant of a man, more attuned to the quiet life of a university campus than the Antarctic but also a man with the nerve and the backbone to see any project through to its end. There was Charlie Murphy, quiet, contemplative, intelligent and tough of mind. There were Dyer, one of the radio men—resourceful, bright; Harold June, the flyer, proved veteran and companion of many expeditions; and George Noville, also a flyer and veteran administrator of the North Pole flight. And of course, the oldest friend of all—Bill Haines.

"Gentlemen," said Byrd, "It is obvious that three men cannot man Advance Base."

They nodded. Dr. Poulter drew deeply on his pipe, and looked at Byrd curiously. "How about two?"

Byrd shook his head. "It is doubtful if it could be supplied even for two. And besides— two men would be at each other's throats in no time."

This was true. Three was the classic number. Living like bugs on pins before their comrades' eyes, there was no privacy of any kind. They would scarcely be able to leave the shack for an hour or two each day, often not even this. Imaginary wrongs would grow huge. Two men could easily sink into a morbid bitter contemplation of each other that would end in disaster. It had happened before. Byrd had seen it happen even in the relatively spacious and well organized confines of Little America. The third man was essential. He provided the balance, the pivot, the arbitrator about which the other two would spin like satellites in orbit. The positions of each man would of course, change from day to day, but no matter how frequent or how temporary was the alignment, there was always the third man to restore balance and sanity.

"Then that leaves one," said Murphy quietly.

"That's right, Charlie," said Byrd.

"And who?" someone murmured.

"I'm going myself," said Byrd.

There was complete silence. Far off in the distance the Barrier creaked and groaned softly. The wind hummed in the ventilator.

"Your mind's made up?" asked Dr. Poulter.

"Quite."

"You've considered it carefully no doubt," said Poulter calmly. "There are many aspects."

Byrd wearily ran his hand through his hair. He had considered nothing else the past few weeks. How could he ask— or order—another man to undertake such a mission?

"How about public opinion back home, Dick?" asked Murphy.

Byrd made a negative gesture. Public opinion! Of course. People would say he had abandoned his position of leadership. He and the men of Little America knew better.

What if some disaster overtook Little America? He would be disgraced forever. He would be like the captain of a ship who abandoned it as the vessel sunk beneath the waves. This he would have to risk. Besides, he had no fears on this score. Little America was a tough ship—manned by as hard-bitten a crew as could be found. These adventurers, explorers, tough seamen, strong-fibred scientists would know how to take care of themselves.

"We'll survive what people back in the States say, Charlie," answered Byrd.

He passed them a slip of paper. Dr. Poulter was to be in command of Little America while he was gone, Bill Haines next in command, Harold June the chief officer, and George Noville the executive officer.

"There's not much more to be said then," Dr. Poulter remarked, "except the inevitable comment, how about yourself? Will you be all right?"

Byrd smiled. "I'll manage. Don't worry about me." He stood up. "One thing more I want to make clear. And this is an order: If you don't hear from me, if you suspect something is wrong at Advance Base, you are not to organize a relief expedition during the night. You are not to endanger the lives of any men because of me. I cannot make this clear enough. No matter what happens, you are not to strike out onto the Barrier until the night is over."

Poulter smiled. "That's clear enough, Dick."

The others murmured assent.

"And now," Byrd said, "I want to write out some last instructions." The men took the hint and filed out quietly. "Charlie," Byrd called after Murphy, "Will you come back a bit later, please? There are some personal matters I would like you to handle for me."

Haines was the last to leave. He turned to Byrd, his honest face crinkled with doubt and worry. "Dick," he said, "You don't have to do this. Those meteorological records are not worth taking such a chance."

Haines was a very old and very close friend. Byrd answered him with great honesty. "Bill," he said, "Let's not pretend. I'm fully aware of the value of the records, but I'm not doing this for science alone."

Haines' face was sober. "I didn't think so, Dick. What is it then?"

Byrd hesitated a moment, then looked his friend full in the eyes. The words were hard to find. How does any man expose what is in his own heart, and most of all, when he himself isn't quite sure of his motives.

"Maybe . . . maybe just because the challenge is there, waiting for me, Bill. Perhaps that's the only reason. Or perhaps I just want to be by myself for a while. To look into myself. To taste one final emotional experience to the full. Completely on my own. I want to know what's really inside me, Bill. Can you understand this?"

"Yes, Dick," Bill Haines said gently. "I think I do. One last hurdle to go over. By yourself."

Byrd was astonished at the man's understanding.

"And Dick," said Haines, "I envy you."

For many hours Byrd stayed up drafting final instructions. His message to the men of the expedition was brief but to the point. It ended with: "every man in this camp has a right to be treated fairly and squarely, and the officers are requested to keep this fact in mind. In a sense our status is primitive . . . We hold no class distinctions as in civilization . . ."

By morning all the loose ends were tied off. The camp buzzed with the news. As Byrd, parka-clad, strode out to the plane, he shook hands all around and climbed in to a chorus of shouts of encouragement and wishes for good luck. The last thing he heard as the door slammed behind him was from the camp cook who yelled cheerfully, "Remember, no class distinctions at Advance Base!"

Grinning broadly, Byrd signaled the pilot and with a roar and a flashing cloud of snow, the skis shook clear and the plane was in the air.

The plane swooped broad and low in a climbing turn over Little America. With almost a choke in his throat, Byrd took in at one last sweeping glance the sprawling, smoke-spewing city he had created.

The plane headed south, over the Barrier.

CHAPTER 10

THE OCCUPATION

A QUICK GLANCE TO THE NORTH REVEALED THAT THE Ross Sea was frozen solid to the horizon. Any danger to Little America from disintegration of the Barrier was past. The Barrier was hard as steel—nothing could move or stir it now for many months.

Heading to the south, the plane picked up the trail of flags left by Innes-Taylor's party weeks before. The bright orange flags fluttered from their bamboo staffs every third of a mile. Every 25 miles there was a tall snow beacon topped by a flag, marking a supply cache. From these caches, another line of flags drove out east and west for a mile on either side—guidelines for any hard-pressed party searching and groping through a blizzard.

Following the flag trail were the tracks of the tractors, like welts on the smooth surface of the snow.

Sixty-seven miles out, the plane swooped low over the stalled tractor. Two mechanics crawled out from under a canvas hood, interrupting their work for a moment to wave a greeting.

Not long after, a dark minute cluster of tents came into view. This was a party already engaged in setting up Advance Base.

Bolling Advance Weather Base, for such was the formal title of the base, lay on a vast windswept plain of ice as enormous as the endless steppes of Siberia, and far colder. The incredible size of the ice plateau seemed all the bigger, all the more empty and lonely because of the puny scratchings of the men below.

One hundred and twenty three statue miles from Little America, Advance Base would be completely inaccessible during the Antarctic night. No life stirred, no living thing of any kind existed in the bitter cold. There was nothing... nothing... not even the smallest plant, a bit of moss... not the tiniest microscopic bacteria would share this frozen world with him. He was truly alone.

The plane landed on March 22. Quickly Byrd jumped from the plane. His sleeping bag, a few odds and ends of personal gear were bumbled out after him, and the plane again took off. The pilot did not dare stop the engine, nor even slow it to idling speed for more than a few moments. The air was so cold it would have frozen and possibly have refused to start again.

Byrd watched the plane soar off until it was a tiny speck against the sky, the vapor from the exhaust trailing like a long graceful feather.

He was soon pumping the hands of Siple, Tinglof, and other members of the base-laying party who came to greet him.

"How is it going?" Byrd asked Siple.

Siple shook his head. "Very slow."

Looking at him, and the rest, Byrd could see why. The cold was bitter, numbing, causing all the life in them to cringe back on itself seeking to preserve heat, slowing the vital processes, making it an agonized effort to work. The evidence of their struggle was all too apparent in the yellow scabs of frostbite on their faces and in their cracked and split lips which from the depths of the fur parkas spread in sorry grins.

Byrd was very pleased to find Captain Innes-Taylor and his party at the site. Racing back to Little America through the shortening days and lengthening nights, they had arrived at Advance Base just in time to lend a hand.

He was, however, regretful at having to delay their return to Little America. They had been through a very rough time. Very low temperatures had dogged them during the entire trip, and what was worse, they had been plagued by defective zippers on their sleeping bags. To rest more than a few minutes at a time had been out of the question during the long journey. Lying still in the half-opened bags would have meant freezing to death. In the mornings, the bags had been so stiff with ice that they had to be pounded in order to roll them up.

A pit big enough to take the shack bodily had been excavated in the ice. Already the floor sections were being fitted in place. Luckily, the shack had been designed for quick assembly, but even so, the job took time. All through the day they worked, as they were desperate for shelter.

By late afternoon, the temperature had sagged into the minus 50s. Their breath made a continuous fog in the pit and the workers coughed incessantly. The exertion made them all breathe more deeply than usual, and the super-cold air tortured their lungs.

At nightfall the walls of the shack were in place, but it was not yet roofed. They struggled on by the light of kerosene lanterns and flashlights. When the temperature worked its way down into the 60s, the flashlights and lanterns went dead. Batteries and kerosene were frozen!

Tinglof found two gasoline blowtorches and managed to get them lit. By this feeble blue glow, and with the heat playing directly on their legs, the men were able to continue to work.

Before nails could be driven or bolts turned they had to be heated. The cold had made them so brittle that they broke under the stroke of a hammer or the twist of a wrench. To save time, the nails and bolts were thawed by a very simple method, holding them in a bare hand. Before long, fingers and palms were stripped of flesh, burned into great yellow blisters by the searing cold.

The roof was finally on by 1 o'clock in the morning. The thermometer registered 63 degrees below zero!

The stovepipes and ventilators were hooked up in short order, and soon Siple had the stove burning. None too soon. Men cannot live and work in such a low temperature. They crowded wearily about the stove, trying to soak up the feeble heat which it was beginning to give off.

Innes-Taylor remarked casually, "I think my foot is frozen."

It was. As soon as he stripped off his mukluks, Byrd tried to massage it back to life with his hands, but the job was useless.

There is an old story that a frozen or frostbitten part of the human body can be thawed in the Antarctic by rubbing it with snow. This is an old wives' tale—spread by people who have never had to survive in such cold. At 63 degrees below zero, snow is granulated, hard. Just as well to have rubbed the foot with sandpaper, with disastrous results. Polar explorers know a better way.

Paine, one of Innes-Taylor's men, unbuttoned his windproof jacket and opened the furs of his parka. Innes-Taylor lay down on the floor and slipped his foot into the pit of Paine's stomach. In fifteen or twenty minutes, the foot revived. The blood swept back into it in a torrent. As it did so, the jolts of pain brought sweat to Innes-Taylor's face. Men in such surroundings learn that their own lives and safety are in the hands of their comrades.

Sleeping bags were brought below, and soon the exhausted crew stretched out to rest. The moment the fire was extinguished, cold again crashed on the shack with the impact of a piledriver.

"Dick, you'll freeze solid in this pit," somebody remarked cheerfully from the cozy warmth of his sleeping bag.

Byrd knew better. He had lived in the shack at Little America. Tight and snug, it would be warm and comfortable as soon as the frost went out of the walls. He had great respect for the way Tingloff had constructed the building. It would serve him well—conserving heat and fending off the worst blows that the Barrier could offer.

By morning the men were awakened by the cheerful beep-beep of the tractors which were returning with the load from the stalled machine. Considering they had been up all night, the tractor crews were in good shape. One good look at them, though, and it was more than apparent what they had been through.

They looked like ragged and pitiful scarecrows. Torn and dirty windproofs, stiff with frozen oil and grease, flapped about their bodies. Their hands were burned and shriveled by the frozen steel which they had worked with. Their nails were burned black and were falling from their fingers; blood dripped from agonizing blisters.

Desperate for the men to be on their way home to Little America, Byrd drove them hard. With the winter night coming on and with temperatures as low as they were, this was no time for crews to be on the trail.

In addition to the ominous weather, there was also the question of the reliability of the tractors. One was already hopelessly broken down and could not be extricated until the following spring. The other two had behaved well enough, but mechanization in the Antarctic was still an unknown quantity. Engines burned out, radiators had a terrible habit of boiling and exploding even in the coldest weather, gears made brittle by the cold cracked and broke. He was glad that on the run back to Little America, the tractors would be backed up by Innes-Taylor and the reliable dog teams. The difference between major disaster and success often hung by such fragile threads in the Antarctic.

The work was fairly well along by now, thanks to the additional help of the returned tractor crews. Actually, only one major task remained.

The pit had been purposefully dug too wide for the shack to

the extent of the overhang or eave of the roof. A sort of vestibule, or "veranda," under the ice was thus formed. From each end of this veranda, two tunnels were dug, parallel to each other. They were about 35 feet long and were to contain the supplies and equipment which Byrd would need over the seven months which lay ahead of him. Each tunnel was three feet wide and deep enough for a man to walk erect. One tunnel contained the fuel, and the other, his food.

As the gear dropped underground, Byrd and Siple made a rough inventory. The quantities and the variety necessary for one man were really astonishing: 350 candles, 3 flashlights, lanterns, batteries, 425 boxes of matches, toothpicks, stoves, pencils, toilet paper, buckets, rubber bands, writing paper, dehydrated and canned vegetables, seal meat, soup, dried and canned fruit, cereals, and many, many other things.

Advance Base was a Little America, but in miniature. Instead of having to provide for 56 men, it would have to be stocked for one only. But except for quantity, and certain items, such as a machine shop, the requirements were the same. Siple, an expert at logistics, which means the supplying of an expedition or party in the field, had figured and planned long over the list. Byrd's fingers were crossed that nothing had been forgotten.

Every item was checked off as the supplies were unloaded from the tractors and sledges and heaved below. Meantime the radio technician set up the communicating apparatus. The antenna was about 200 feet long and was strung on four tall bamboo poles on the top of the Barrier. Bamboo was always used for such things—antennae, flag markers and so on—because it would bend and whip in the wind without breaking. The transmitter and receiver were tested and worked perfectly. Byrd also had available to him two 10-watt emergency transmitters operated by a crank as well as two stand-by receivers with their own batteries. The main transmitter had been made at Little America by the radio unit and consisted of a 50-watt self-excited oscillator. The main receiver was a good super-heterodyne.

When the supplies were finally checked and stored, Byrd and Siple took time to set up the meteorological equipment. There was a great deal of it, because Advance Base was designed to do a thorough job.

By the end of the second day, the base was completed and ready to go as the world's southernmost weather station.

That night, in celebration, and also as a farewell banquet for Innes-Taylor's dog-sledge party, a feast was held. The Supply Officer had thoughtfully included in Byrd's larder a turkey and two chickens. After considerable fast-talking by the men, Byrd donated them for the dinner. The poultry was frozen hard as granite boulders but this was only a minor deterrent for the resourceful tractor men; they thawed the birds with blowtorches. The banquet was a big success.

That night the dog drivers slept outside in their tents while the other men stretched out in the shack in their sleeping bags. There was hardly room to move without stepping on someone.

During the night the wind mounted and a blinding blizzard came yelling down out of the south. Though buffeted and battered, the shack took the storm in stride, but there could be no thought of the crews getting away the next day. The blizzard continued all the day and the next night.

Driven outside by the thunderous snoring of his "guests," Byrd took a brief walk for a look at the weather. Through the swirling drift he went to check on the dogs. The three teams were tethered in parallel lines to a steel wire strung between gee poles hammered into the snow crust. Each dog was curled up in a tight ball, back to the wind and muzzle tucked into his belly. The drift fanned out to the leeward of each animal, lie the wake of a ship at sea.

During a lull in the wind the driving drift slackened, and as Byrd looked up through the scud of clouds he caught a glimpse of the deep blue Antarctic sky, glittering with stars. He guessed the weather might be improving.

Now a strange thing happened. Jack, the great lead dog of the teams suddenly heaved himself to his feet, shook the snow from his back. He sniffed the air, then pointed his muzzle to the sky and over the Barrier rose the wild cry of a wolf-dog. Instantly all twenty-four dogs were on their feet, joining the eery wail. It was a wail of hunger and of lust and of deep instinct. They knew somehow that the morning would see them on the trail. They welcomed the task.

The Huskies were right. Morning dawned clear and cold. Innes-Taylor got off, and a bit later one of the small tractors left with the crew and mechanics who would make a final efforts to salvage the stalled machine.

The others lingered just long enough to make everything shipshape. They lingered also with the strange reluctance of men who are loathe to leave a comrade whom they will not see for many months, a comrade whose life during this time will not be easy and may even be in danger.

They tested the radio equipment again. Tinkered with the stove. Checked the meteorological gear. How do you manage such a leavetaking? What are the words to be said?

In the middle of lunch, Harold June suddenly remarked very casually, "Well, we've done just about everything that needs doing, and a lot of things I suspect that needed no doing at all, so I guess it's time to shove off."

As simply as this the problem of good-byes was solved!

But it was not good-bye, after all. In two hours the last of the two tractors was back. The radiator on June's machine had boiled. In trying to unscrew the cap to feed it snow, he had scalded one hand in the geyser of steam, and frozen the other trying to nurse it. After the burns were taken care of, it was too late to make another departure, so the crew stayed the night. The engines were kept idling until morning. If they stopped it would have meant long hours thawing them with a blowtorch.

At noon on the following day, the tractors took their final departure.

Byrd watched them go, their cabs a jaunty and cheerful red against the white of the snow. The vapor from the exhausts rose high in the still air and hung over them like a gleaming spire.

Alone at last, Byrd went below to look at what would be his home for many months. Suddenly the place was empty and more than a little lonely. The shack which had seemed so bright and cheery when filled with the voices of many men, was now cold and dead.

Obeying a sudden impulse, he rushed up the ladder, out the trapdoor, and stood gazing after his comrades. The cars were some distance away now, barely small dots in the immensity, over which hung the vaporous clouds of their exhausts. Even at this distance, however, he could hear the beep-beep of their horns and the clatter of their treads over the packed snow.

He watched until they vanished behind a long, rolling rise in the Barrier. There was no sound of life left. Nothing remained but the tall columns of the tractors' breathing, which rose straight up into the clean sky.

With their going, the world of men, of companionship, shrank to nothing. With this, the ancient ice-age world rose about him—grim, overpowering. Out of the lowering sky to the south, a giant seemed grimly to take his measure.

A frozen nose and cheek sent him scurrying below.

Richard was truly alone.

CHAPTER 11

A PERSONAL CHALLENGE

NOW BEGAN ONE OF THE STRANGEST VIGILS EVER KEPT by a human being. Its story is one of the most illuminating documents of personal courage and honor ever written about a man.

Ahead of Byrd lay seven months of isolation; a number of them would be in the darkness of nights 24 hours long. Except for occasional radio contacts with the base at Little America, he would be as remote from the assistance, the warmth, and the companionship of his fellows as he might be if marooned on a planet in space.

Alone in his tiny shack sunk deep in the ice of the glacier, it was up to Byrd alone to make his own life tolerable, comfortable, and safe.

Over the insignificant pin-prick which was Advance Base brooded the great giant of the Antarctic. This implacable, mortal foe waited with infinite patience for Byrd to make a false step, a mistake. For such a mistake there would be no forgiveness, no second chance.

Byrd must match the resources of this enemy with his own patience and cunning. Never could he be contemptuous or guilty of underestimating the power of this adversary, which he knew so well. However, the human mind can only remain sensitive to anything for so long. A constantly repeated threat finally loses meaning. Repetition saps the mind, dulls its awareness, makes a man careless of his guard.

Complete, unthinking obedience to safety rules had been drilled by Byrd into his men, and into himself, for years, until they had become as much a part of him as breathing. Upon this ingrained, disciplined, carefully nurtured trait his survival depended throughout the months which lay ahead.

As he settled down to arrange his life into a routine, it seemed to him that there were three deadly sources of danger which stood out above all others.

One was injury or illness. How can a man be sure that he won't have an accident? That he won't hurt himself? He can't, of course, but precautions can be taken. Like the constant admonition of a mother to a young child to "watch for cars before you cross the street," Byrd told himself to watch what he did. He was careful in the thousand and one daily activities, large and small, to take no undue chances. As for illness—he was in superb physical health and in one respect, Antarctica is a paradise. There are no germs.

A second source of danger was fire. If the hut ever caught fire, nothing could save it. And so again, he was careful always. Not just when he thought about it, but subconsciously, all the time. If this disaster should strike, he had a complete trail outfit—food, tent, cooker, and other equipment stowed at the far end of one of the tunnels. With it he might conceivably get through the winter if the shack were to be destroyed.

The third great danger, and the one of which Byrd was most aware, was getting lost on the surface of the Barrier. In calm weather and foul, it was necessary for him to go topside and tend the weather instruments. Drift snow collected on the anemometer cups, rime on various contact points—all of which had to be scraped away so the recordings would be accurate. In addition to this, a small slatted box on stilts housed various thermometers which had to be read. Although these instruments were all located within a few feet of the trapdoor entrance, and Byrd knew their bearings perfectly, the blizzards were sometimes so thick and fierce that he literally could not see his hand before his eyes, and would be completely turned around and lost after a step or two.

Furthermore, a certain amount of exercise was absolutely necessary; he tried to continue his life-long habit of taking walks. North and south of the trapdoor he marked out a path and strung bamboo sticks along it. Eventually, so rapidly and thickly did the storms descend that Byrd hung a lifeline along these stakes and many times this thin cord between his fingers led him to safety out of a howling, dark chaos.

The shack in a sense was like a small fortress defending Byrd's life against the enemy. In dozens of ways, each day, he inspected and strengthened its defenses. Ice and rime was picked out of the ventilator pipes. He worked on an emergency exit in case a prolonged blow piled the drift so high he would be unable to get out the trapdoor. He stowed emergency rations and fuel in the shack itself so that if he became ill or crippled and unable to get to the tunnels, supplies would be near at hand.

Slowly life settled into a routine pattern for him. Like the ordered whirling of the sun and stars and planets in the sky overhead, his existence assumed a rhythm and order.

The sun, like a glowing ball of pure molten gold, rolled along the edge of the horizon. Each day it peeped up for a shorter and shorter time and the twilights became longer and longer. Finally the sun, as if unable to lift itself above the horizon, left only the afterglow of where it had been. Night had come. Except for these fleeting twilights, there was no light except that given by the stars swimming through the crowded, populous sky, and by the moon—a weird mysterious ball which rolled through the heavens—now green, now blue, now orange.

Outside on the Barrier, the Antarctic, like an evil spirit, brooded, ready to pounce. Its lurking presence colored Byrd's entire existence. Inside the shack, dimly lit by kerosene lanterns, his life was governed by the clocks of the weather-recording mechanisms. Their demands ruled him. Time was the master; he the slave.

In addition to his simple housekeeping, Byrd actually had a great deal of work to do. Meteorological observations occupied a considerable part of each day. The instruments on the outside had to be kept in working order and the readings constantly noted. The clockwork mechanisms of other instruments inside the hut had to be wound each day, the graphs changed, and the pens refilled with ink.

In addition to this, there were twice-daily notings to be made on the state of cloudiness and the weather in general. Whenever the skies were clear he made five daily auroral observations.

And so, Byrd's life sunk into an orderly routine. Not the useless routine of futility, but a merging of the job he had to perform with the great world of nature.

He worked on the escape tunnel, cooked, read, took daily walks, tended his instruments. He doled out the time so as to space the hours, fill them all with activity of some type. This was really the only defense a man could erect against the loneliness and the brain-eroding monotony of his existence.

As time passed, there were things which arose and which plagued him to such an extent that he had to summon all his powers of resistance to combat them.

Light for example. Just plain ordinary light. Man is a creature of the light, of the sun. Although he may love the night with its mystery and beauty and poetry, he does so in the sure knowledge that with the dawn in the morning, the sun will flood the earth with radiance.

There was no such release for Byrd. There would be no sun tomorrow. There was no bright room waiting for him under the snow. As time went on this became more and more of a problem. He craved light as a drowning man craves air. The storm lantern cast only a dim glow which barely chased the shadows into the corners of the room. Finally, driven by sheer necessity, he fell into the habit of lighting the gasoline pressure lamp for an hour or two in the evenings. Its light was brilliant, dazzling white. He used the lamp sparingly because it consumed a large amount of gasoline and gave off unpleasant fumes. The brief time it was lit, however, was very precious to him. Every fiber of his body drank in the light thirstily.

A great peace descended upon him, when his whole being was in total harmony and agreement with the great universe which spun majestically through the skies overhead. There were times though, when the awesome dangers of his existence crashed through to him with grim warning: Do not relax, do not be lulled for an instant. The price for forgetfulness is high. No matter how much his mind sank down into itself, no matter how much it craved the oblivion of routine, he forced himself to discipline his life and his activities to wakefulness. He must never become unaware of the fearsome capabilities of his world.

But there were times . . . when forgetfulness took over . . .

The twilight was beautiful. The horizon was a long slash of purest scarlet. The sky swarmed with stars, and a thin, ethereal haze drifted between earth and heaven. For the sake of "variety" he had walked out along the radio antenna line. Just beyond the last pole—fifty or sixty feet beyond—he had planted a bamboo marker to serve as a beacon. As he stood there, thinking about nothing in particular, perhaps just soaking up the beauty of the night, Byrd suddenly remembered he had violated one of his cardinal rules: he had left the stove burning when he went topside.

Quickly he turned, started back toward the trapdoor which

was a few hundred feet distant. Worried about the possibility of fire, he hurried, his face buried deeply in his parka against the wind, and paying no attention to where he stepped.

Suddenly he was hurled sideways, as though a giant had clubbed him from behind. When he came to, some time later, he was sprawled flat on the snow, legs dangling over an open crevasse.

Inch by inch, lest he break the ledge loose, he crept, scarcely breathing. When his wits returned, he crawled back for a look. A great pit yawned beneath him, bottomless, shimmering under the beam of his flashlight. The crevasse was bridged over by a thin layer of snow and ice. Luckily, he had crossed it at right angles; otherwise he would have plunged to certain death.

Thoroughly chastened, he went below, got several bamboo sticks, returned to the crevasse and marked it clearly.

Woolgathering, daydreaming . . . there was the danger, the enemy. He had come within an inch of losing his life in one sudden, jarring fall.

Another time, in a very fine mood, at ease with himself and the world which wheeled so beautifully in the night above him, Byrd decided to take a longer walk than usual.

The Barrier was dark, the wind blowing steadily, causing drift to waft gently through the air. Parading up and down his lifeline, Byrd's mind soon lost itself in imagination. Always fascinated by the unending expanse of the ice cap over the continent of the Antarctic, he fell to speculating as to how the whole world must have looked when the earth was young. The ice advancing, retreating, driving before it men and all other life. Perhaps some day when the sun was old and tired and our earth was in the twilight of its years, once again the ice would advance. And perhaps the last men on earth would live, eke out their days, just as Byrd lived now. Perhaps . . . perhaps . . .

The wind was rising, the drift increasing. He turned to go back to the hut, the thought of warm food, light, drawing him like a magnet.

The line of bamboo sticks was nowhere in sight!

The thin beam of his flashlight probed through the swirling drift to pick out . . . nothing. In his abstraction, Byrd had wandered beyond his lifeline!

Stunned by the enormity of his predicament, Byrd's first impulse was to run! But where? Even his footsteps were invisible on the hard snow.

He beat down the panic in his mind and took stock of the situation. The wind had been on his left cheek when he started his walk. This much he remembered, but it meant little. Suppose the wind had veered?

What must a navigator have to get from one place to another? A point of departure and a direction to follow, a range. Before anything else, Byrd was a navigator—one of the best in the world.

With his heel he scratched up a little mount of snow. The sky had cleared somewhat so by lining up a couple of stars, he had a direction to follow.

Taking carefully paced steps, he started forward. One hundred steps. He played the beam of the light over the Barrier. Nothing.

He did not dare go farther for fear of losing his one known point: the pitiful little snow beacon. Retreating, he counted off another hundred steps, and with deep apprehension, turned on the light. Nothing. He stood on the thin edge of panic again, a dark and insignificant fur clad figure lost in the immensity of sky and snow. Then the light picked up the beacon 20 feet or so to his left.

Byrd made several more stabs into the blackness, each time in a slightly different direction. Still nothing.

He realized he would have to lengthen his radius from the beacon, but in so doing he might very well lose the miserable snow hummock. There was no alternative. Death from freezing would not be long coming and it could happen just as easily 500 yards from the hut as it could 50 yards away.

So again, he paced off 100 steps and marked this point with another little pile of snow. The wind drifted pitilessly; darkness and cold were close at hand. Again quelling deep animal panic, he continued on for another 30 steps. On the last pace, the flick of light picked up a bamboo marker.

Byrd closed his eyes. Warm relief surged through him and a prayer of thanks formed in his heart. This had been too close. Never again did he allow himself to dream, to be forgetful of what lay in wait for him.

Time moved along, slowly and inexorably. In a thousand little tricks and stunts he devised ways to fill the time, to keep busy, to keep his mind from succumbing to the monotony. He read, thought, brooded, contemplated himself—Richard Evelyn Byrd. Who was he? What did he mean? What was his life worth?

In spite of all his efforts, however, he found that he was sinking into a pit of depression, an ennui which took possession of him. Byrd fought these moods with every ounce of his strength. He talked himself into feeling better. "It must be psychological," he thought.

He reviewed his way of living. There was no reason for feeling so poorly. One day up. Another day down. Mentally he examined every aspect of his life. Plenty of sleep. Plenty of exercise. His diet was simple, but it contained sufficient vitamins and energy-giving foods. He blamed his dark feelings on the lack of companionship. After all, a man may crave solitude, may wish with all his heart for the opportunity to be alone for a time and think, examine himself. Nevertheless, all the fabric of our existence, the fine-spun web of our daily lives is largely made up of contacts with other people. There were none for him.

Physically he felt fairly well except for nagging headaches. Dredging deeply into the depths of his will, Byrd managed to keep on a fairly even keel. In spite of a vague uneasiness and a constant irritability with himself, he functioned well enough, did his work, and even found some joy in his life.

He was a queer sight no doubt, but vanity had a no place in the hut at Advance Base. His hair had not been cut for months, and as the weather grew colder, he even gave up trimming the ends. The long growth over neck and ears helped keep him warm! He still shaved once a week—not for the sake of appearance but rather because outside on the Barrier surface a beard tended to ice up from his breath, and freeze solid. His cheeks were blistered from the cold and his nose swollen, red and bulbous from hundreds of frostbites.

Toward the last of May the darkness continued to deepen until his whole world was a pit of darkness at the bottom of an enormous well. The cold dragged lower and lower. On May 20, the thermometer inside the hut registered minus 74 degrees. Minus 74 degrees! The figure gives no inkling of what such a temperature means, just as the pen tracings which record a wind velocity or an earthquake convey no impression of the actuality. The thermograph in the shack which recorded the temperature on the surface was stopped dead. Although well diluted with glycerine, the ink in the pens would not flow. The lubricant in the clockwork mechanisms was hard as stone. Even the fuel for his stove was so stiff it had to be warmed with a blowtorch!

After a miserable day of nursing the instruments, he felt for the first time really ill. His body was wracked with shooting pains. A foot which had become frozen when he went topside to tend the instruments throbbed steadily. For the radio schedule with Little America, he had to carry the generator in and stand it by the stove to thaw before it would start. When he finally got on the air he was so tired he could scarcely work the key. The voices floated gently to him out of the north. Dyer, the radio operator, was as always calm and courteous. Haines, the meteorologist, was jolly and joking as he gave instructions on how to get the instruments functioning again. Charlie Murphy was calm, quizzical, assaying as he always seemed to do, Byrd's thoughts and comments. He was worn out when the schedule was over and was grateful for a warm supper and the comfort of his sleeping bag.

Then, out of the unbearable cold came a blizzard. Slowly the wind rose, sobbing in the ventilators, shaking the stovepipe, pounding the roof of the shack with tremendous jarring blows.

The wind continued to rise, finally reaching gale force. The very glacier seemed to tremble beneath its furious impact.

The wind-direction pen turned scratchy on the graph, oscillating violently. The flailing drift above had no doubt short-circuited the electrical contacts. For a while Byrd judged wind direction by holding a bit of rag on a stick through the ventilator pipe and noting with a flashlight the way it streamed. By two in the morning he had had enough of this and resolved to go topside and clean the contacts.

He plunged into an infernal nightmare. Drift snow; which in the intense cold was frozen to the hardness of sand, tore at him with a million icy claws, clogging his mouth, nostrils and lungs.

He came out the trapdoor, head buried in his parka, afraid to stand erect. If the wind caught him, he would be thrown off his feet, all sense of direction would be gone and he would be forever lost.

He found the pole, but not until his head had collided with it. He managed to climb it, too, but the errand was useless. Drift such as this would foul the contact points again in an instant, and besides, he stood to lose his fingers in the crazily whirling anemometer.

Noting carefully the direction to the hatch trapdoor, he crawled back, found it.

It was tightly shut, and as he pulled at the handle, it refused to budge. "The drift has probably wedged the corners," he mumbled to himself.

Standing erect, he pulled at the handle with all his strength. He might just as well have tried to lift the shack itself.

And now, for the first time, panic did master him. He beat on the door like a madman, clawing at it. For months he had strengthened his fortress against the danger of being penned inside it. Now with a horrible perverse humor, the Antarctic had locked him outside. Three feet below him, completely beyond his reach, lay food, warmth—survival. Outside there was literally nothing.

There are few things so insane and vindictive as an Antarctic blizzard. Its enmity is personal. The lungs gasp for air as the wind tears it from them. The skin cringes, crawls. The sound is like a continual explosion, numbing the brain.

Frantically, Byrd went to the ventilator. It was just a few feet away. Like a lost specter he kneeled, peered down. Nothing was visible but a few square feet of floor—so warm, so near and so completely unattainable.

The tiny patch of light steadied him. He could still think. If only he had something to dig with. The stovepipe perhaps would do. Crazily he pulled on it—back and forth, up and down. It was a solid pillar of frozen steel, far beyond his strength.

And then, his mind disciplined, still functioning, he remembered that a week before he had shoveled some drift off the roof and had left the shovel topside. But where? And how to find it in this darkness?

He lay down full length and held on to the stovepipe with his hands, searching with his feet in a wide circle. They encountered nothing.

Then he worked his way to the hatch and repeated the maneuver. Still nothing. His flailing feet did, however, come up hard against the other ventilator. He crawled to it, and again searched in the wide circle. He dared not let go the pipe; once his grip was lost on something familiar, he too would be lost.

This time his feet struck hard against the handle of the shovel. Embracing it as dearly as life itself, he worked his way back to the trapdoor. The haft of the shovel would just fit under the hatch handle. He inserted it and using the leverage, pulled with all his might. The door refused to budge. So he lay down on the ice, flat on his stomach, and squirmed under the shovel handle. Exerting upward every ounce of his strength with his arched back, he heaved. The door sprang open.

He rolled down the ladder, into the warmth and light below like a man tossed up on a beach by the breakers. For a long time, just gasping, he lay weakly on the floor of the vestibule. When his strength returned, he crawled up the ladder, slammed the trapdoor shut and returned to the shack.

On May 31, there was a long radio schedule with Little America. Still weak and shaken, so he thought, from his narrow escape from death on the surface, he managed to make contact with the base. There were many problems to consider. Many decisions to make. Only he, the leader, could make them. Messages to representatives back in the States concerning money matters and the dwindling expedition treasury. (Crazy thought this one—money matters. What did money have to do with him here in a pit on the glacier!) A long talk with Dr. Poulter and Charlie Murphy regarding the proposed spring expeditions. His injunctions to them: Be careful of crevasses, check the deviation of the compasses in the planes. He suggested that they engage an ice pilot for the *Jacob Ruppert* when she returned through the ice pack to the Bay of Whales. And so it went. Wearily, with a mounting headache, with increased irritability with himself, Byrd got through an hour and a half discussion with the base.

Suddenly, to his intense annoyance, the faithful little generator in the tunnel started missing and sputtering. The voltage meters on the transmitter jerked up and down.

He tapped out the signal for "wait" on the key, took the storm lantern and went into the tunnel. It was filled with the blue, gassy fog of the exhaust. Thinking the mixture was at fault, he bent to adjust the carburetor. Then suddenly, like a stunned ox, Byrd blacked out.

Some time later, like a voice calling in a dream, a voice insisted to him that something important had to be done. What needed doing, he wasn't quite sure. The cold roused him sufficiently to crawl back into the shack. The radio desk emerged in a blue haze, and he tapped out something on the key. If there was any acknowledgement, he didn't hear. He could not get the earphones on.

[The radio log at Little America shows that 20 minutes elapsed between the time he said "wait" and the time he signed off saying "see you next Sunday." This is the time that he was unconscious on the floor of the tunnel.]

Some part of his brain still worked. He knew he had been overcome by fumes. He knew the generator must be shut off. Again, crawling on the floor, he reached the hammering, clattering little engine through a haze of poisonous fog, and shut it down.

After another eternity, or so it seemed, he crawled back into the shack, pushing the storm lantern ahead of him. He inched over to the bunk. Nothing was real—only the cold which gnawed at his bones. He must get warm!

In the face of stabbing pain in his head, his heart throbbing weakly and violently like a butterfly's wings, unbearable nausea, he managed to crawl up on his bunk where he lay panting for long minutes. Finally he was able to grasp the flap of his sleeping bag and slide his tortured body inside.

He knew no more.

CHAPTER 12

THE STRUGGLE
FOR SURVIVAL

JUNE 1. THE BEGINNING NIGHTMARE.

After a lifetime spent in the far and dangerous places of the earth, Byrd now embarked on his most intense struggle for survival. He had to mobilize all his scant resources for this assault on his own weakness and frailty.

Time—the days and weeks and months which followed his collapse—lay ahead of him like a long thin thread which was pulled excruciatingly tight, like a taut violin string, twisted far past the breaking point. The slightest jar, the most minute pull would cause it to snap, and with the breaking, time would stop, would have run out to the end.

The clock stood at nine in the morning when Byrd awoke and dragged himself up from the black pit of the tortured night.

With his mind groping through the dark shadows, he painfully examined his situation.

He looked at the stove, standing cold and silent in the middle of the room. The source of warmth and heat, it was also his deadliest enemy. Bit by bit, throughout the past few months, it had silently poisoned him. Siple was right. The leaky joints in the pipe, the loose lid and door, the cracks— slowly they had released small amounts of carbon monoxide into the air he breathed. The heavy dose he had taken in the tunnel had been the final blow.

He knew that this kind of monoxide poison was a deadly and relentless thing. It slowly destroyed tissue in the body, insidiously attacked the deep vital organs, wore down a man's ability to recover. Silently he looked at his stove. It was a good friend who had betrayed him. The irritability, the annoying headaches, the unevenness of his well-being, all had been warning signals which he had not heeded.

Weakly, Byrd's head dropped back on the bunk. Two facts seemed clear. The chances of recovery in any case were very slight. Here, unable to take care of himself, they appeared to be nil.

But he must have faith, and hope, he told himself. This is the ultimate, despairing cry of every man who has started on a dangerous journey from which there is no turning back. A prayer for hope when there is no reason for hope.

As he lay in his bunk thinking, little by little his soul seemed to be stripped bare. He was revealed to himself for what he was. The values he held did not seem important at this time. A tremendous, agonizing blow of pure truth came to him—the unpretentious, homely things of life are the important ones.

He had come to Advance Base looking for peace and for the chance to find some truth, something perhaps to enrich him, make him more useful. What he had sought had been in front of his eyes all the time. What he had done seemed now just a vain pretension.

The excuse to the world? A scientific mission? Ridiculous. A martyr for science? Absurd. He thought of the slowly growing pile of scientific data which he had accumulated. What did he really know about it? There were others far more qualified than he to collect and evaluate such information.

Wearily he forced his mind to stop thinking. In slow motion he got out of bed. Impelled by a raging thirst, he went to the vestibule and like a dog, lapped a few mouthfuls of snow. He crawled back to the stove; after an interminable time finally succeeded in lighting it. Then he passed out.

When he awoke, his parka sleeves were frozen to the wood of the table. He lay his head down on crossed arms and wept, sobbing out the bitter tears of final remorse. "What a pity, what a pity," went the refrain through his spirit.

And with the words, something still left in him seemed to stand to one side and look at him: Admiral Richard Evelyn Byrd, Virginia gentleman, the man who believed it was wrong ever to give way to feelings and emotions. Even his pride now was gone.

But because he was a man—a disciplined, tough-spirited man above all else, some things did remain.

Honor. Responsibility to others. He looked at the little brass key of the radio transmitter. Four letters of the International

Code were all it would take. H-E-L-P. All the resources of Little America would be mobilized to reach him. But even to hint to those for whom he was responsible and set them on a desperate trek across the blizzard-torn glacier was not to be thought of. One hundred and twenty-three miles of snow, storm and crevasse? Sure death for them, and so out of the question.

Courage. Was this really left him? Perhaps yes, and perhaps no. No man wants to die, and will fight off death until the last bitter moment. But is it right to speak of courage when there is no choice? When there is no place left to which a man could run? But perhaps he did have a choice—the final one. He could simply stay in the sleeping bag and die, or he could try to do what needed doing. A bleak, simple, crystal clear choice.

Tick tick tick tick tick tick tick tick tick tick tick went the remorseless little clocks which turned the recording apparatus. They needed winding. The graphs needed changing. For a long time he stared. Then, wracked with nausea, with the knives of pain lashing his body, swaying from weakness, he crawled to the shelves and performed the chores.

Weakly he turned and looked back at his bunk. It seemed a vast, unattainable distance away, but finally he made it and slid into the icy sleeping bag.

A man, even as he lies dying, still thinks. With trembling fingers he lit two candles, found a piece of paper, a pencil. Painfully he wrote a few brief notes. To Dr. Poulter and Charlie Murphy concerning the expedition. A message to the men at Little America. A brief note to his family. These slips of paper he hung over his bunk on a nail, blew out the lights and sunk back into a crazy world of insane dreams and shouting phantoms.

And so miraculously, the days passed. Moments of lucidity when he performed simple tasks, followed by long hours of wandering. Moments when he thought he was dead, followed by moments when he knew that if he didn't manage to wake in the morning he would die for certain.

Heat? Clearly enough, his enemy was the stove. And yet it was his only source of warmth. It must be lit. He lit it only for very brief periods during the day and then always with the door to the tunnels cracked open. But never did he feel warm. Never did the cold leave his bones, and the quiet, dark inner organs crying for heat. Slowly the ice formed on the inside of the shack. First on the floor. Then the walls. Then the ceiling.

Water? His thirst was boundless, but only when he was truly desperate for water did he leave the stove on long enough to melt a few cupfuls of snow.

His stomach clamored for food, but rebelled, threw up even half cups of warmed powdered milk. The floor became spotted with vomit which froze in ugly masses. Only by taking the milk bit by bit—by the spoonful— was he able to keep it down.

But time passed, and somehow, he still lived. Perhaps it was faith alone that kept him alive. He prayed. He reworked in his tortured mind the tenets of his faith, and found after a fashion, words to which he could cling.

But they were just words: "Striving in the right direction for Peace as well as the achievement of it, is the result of accord with a Universal Intelligence." Even as he repeated the words to himself, being a most practical man he knew that to state a faith is one thing, to live it is another. Life for him right now meant food, warmth, light.

Every man has deep wells and reserves of strength which he rarely uses. During this period Byrd dredged far down, scraped the very bottom . . . not only for the will to live, but for the means to accomplish it.

Gradually, ever so slightly, he was on the mend. Or at least it seemed so to him. Perhaps there was no real improvement; perhaps it was only the fact that he was able at times to eat a bit more than tea or warm milk which gave him the feeling that there was a chance for life.

He lived from day to day. The long, long night still stretched far ahead of him. Spring was too distant even to contemplate. It was nearly four months until he could expect help. His own instructions to Little America had been more than explicit on this point. How can a man consider the means for getting through four months when the next hour is in doubt?

But somehow time slowly leaked away in tiny drops of pure burning agony. Tick tick tick tick—the companionable little clatter of the clockwork was a friendly, steady, sane voice, reassuring him that somewhere in the world there was normalcy. But it was also a monster which drove and lashed him without mercy. The readings he kept were his only justification for life, and in obedience to the clocks, he tended them faithfully. Slowly the little pile of data increased.

The worst times were those when he had to keep radio schedules with Little America. They must be kept. He must make a pretense of well-being. The physical wreck which was Richard Byrd must go through the motions of being the leader of a great Antarctic expedition. His men must not become alarmed about him. Luckily, Morse code is impersonal. He was not a really competent operator to begin with, so his ragged sending did not betray him.

But he was also a man, a still-living man. Every atom in his body, during each schedule, cried out in anguish to his fingertips—imploring them to tap out the words to his comrades. Not to do so was hard, the hardest thing he had ever done. He remained true to his resolve and said nothing.

He had to prepare for these contacts hours in advance. The generator weighted 35 pounds and it took much time and strength—a strength far beyond his reserves—to drag it and push it from the tunnel next to the stove for thawing.

These schedules left him exhausted for hours, sometimes for days. The toll they took of his physical power was enormous and the emotional drain was almost more than he could bear.

There were endless problems at Little America. Nothing serious, really, rather just the multitude of small things which only he could handle. Endless discussions, questions from those he had left in charge. Should we do this? Or would it be better to do that? Decisions, decisions, decisions. All of which he tried to answer, never betraying his own pain.

When he tapped out the final "All okay here, cheerio" and signed off, each time it seemed to him that in so doing he was signing for certain his own death certificate.

But even now, in his dire extremity, the disciplines and instincts which had guided him over a lifetime still worked for him. During his "up" moments he dragged extra fuel from the far end of the tunnel into the shack against the day when he might not be able to make it. He brought in cans of food, biscuits, chocolate, powdered milk which he placed within reach on the shelf over his bunk. He managed even to regulate and order his mind and keep from thinking gloomy dark thoughts which seemed to spring by themselves out of the depths of blackness. Despondency became a mortal enemy, attacking his sanity, his will to live. Only by keeping his mind light, out of the darkness, was he able to fight this terror. Only by concentrating on the minute details of each day, each simple task, was he able to keep busy and so retain his sanity.

And so the weeks passed.

Back at Little America, life also moved through its own patterns.

In the under-the-ice city, men passed the time, each in his own way, and each was devoted to the tasks which confronted him. As always, this was the time for planning the big field parties which would start in the latter part of the winter and early spring. The camp hummed with activity.

But there was also something else. A growing suspicion in the mind of one man—Charles Murphy, Byrd's old and good friend. Murphy began to have vague feelings that all was not well at Advance Base.

Murphy stood in the radio shack, Dr. Poulter at his elbow. Dyer was at the typewriter, earphones clamped to his head.

Murphy looked at the paper in the machine, at the words painfully spelled out under the keys. He noted the long pauses, the requests to wait, the seeming incoherencies, the misspelled words.

He turned to Poulter. "There's something wrong, Doc," he said. A cold hard knot formed in the pit of his stomach; this was the first time the vague suspicions had found strength enough to clamor for expression. Now they seemed stronger than ever.

"What do you mean, Charlie?" asked Poulter.

"I don't know what I mean," said Murphy. "I just think something is terribly wrong with Dick."

Dr. Poulter grunted, looked doubtfully at Murphy. "Watch it, Charlie. You'll be ready to set yourself up as a clairvoyant next thing you know."

Murphy paid him no attention. "Dyer," he said during a long pause while they waited for Byrd to resume sending, "Is there anything..." He found the words hard to say. "Is there anything strange about the way the Admiral's sending? How is his fist on the key? Anything... can you put your finger on anything at all?"

Dyer turned his honest face to Murphy. "Can't say there is, Charlie," he replied truthfully. "Dick's pretty bad at best you know."

Murphy indicated the message on the typewriter. "But this?" A long time would be needed to fill in the gaps, to make it read sense.

"He's no operator. That's for sure." Dyer laughed. "He barely knows the code. But you should see some of the stuff other beginners get off."

"But..." Murphy started.

Dyer held up his hand. Byrd had started to send again. Dyer took one of the earphones from the headband, placed it on the desk, so they could all hear. Murphy bent his head as though to read in the very sound of the signal the truth about his friend.

There was nothing but the scraping crash of static and the clean whistle of the dots and dashing ripping through it. Murphy ran his hands through his hair in bewilderment and his face was troubled. There was nothing—nothing to go on.

And yet something inside him was screaming: something is wrong. Terribly, terribly wrong.

The signals whistled and drilled through the clear, cold air. On the typewriter Dyer slowly tapped out their message. "All well. See you on Sunday. Cheerio."

And Dyer, calm and measured, ever courteous, signed off, his voice echoing softly through the shack. "We shall look for you on our regular schedule Sunday next. Good evening, Sir."

Nothing to go on, and yet the doubt remained in Charlie Murphy.

At Advance Base, dying or as close to dying as a man can be who still lives, Byrd hung limply over the key a moment. Then he painfully crawled to the generator, shut it down, returned to the shack, turned off the stove and collapsed in his bunk.

CHAPTER 13

CAUSE FOR CONCERN

AS BYRD FOUGHT HIS SOLITARY BATTLE AT ADVANCE Base, another struggle began to take shape at Little America.

Charlie Murphy could not shake his feeling that there was trouble at Advance Base. As the days passed, this presentiment grew stronger and stronger.

"Doc," he said to Poulter, "This has gone quite far enough. We must do something."

Poulter regarded Murphy silently. He held Murphy in very high esteem; he knew Murphy was not a man to get excited over phantoms. But still . . .

"I . . . I don't know. Why, Charlie?" he asked for the hundredth time. "You have nothing to go on. Or do you?"

"Don't ask me," snapped Murphy. "I only know if we don't take steps soon, it will be too late."

Poulter was a rock of a man, logical and calm, but something of Murphy's jitters began to touch him.

"What can we do, Charlie?" he asked.

Now it was Murphy's turn for despair. "Lord help me, but I don't know." He looked helplessly at his friend. Then his jaw set. "I'm ready to take off across the Barrier right now."

Poulter's reply was only a short laugh.

"Why not?" Murphy's enthusiasm mounted. "The tractors are about ready. They could leave very soon you know."

This was true. During the months which had passed, the mechanics had completely overhauled the machines. Electrical systems were replaced, generators repaired, and treads rebuilt.

In addition, the cabs had been completely re-designed and rebuilt. Great towering wooden structures had been fashioned in which bunks had been placed, together with radio equipment and gasoline heaters. The machines were practically self-contained. They would not only transport their crews but would also furnish them shelter and warmth, as well. They were large and ungainly, and had provoked much joking comment among the men. All agreed however, that they were practical, and this was all that counted.

"Sure, sure, the tractors . . . maybe one of them is ready to go. But are we? You know what it's like out there, Charlie."

Murphy did know. The Antarctic at night was more than dangerous. There was the awful cold, the blizzards. How would it be possible to navigate with no stars visible through the swirling snow? The trail-marker flags would almost certainly be down by now.

139

"I know what it's like," said Murphy stubbornly. "But I'm ready to try."

"Impossible," said Dr. Poulter. "The men would never let a party leave camp right now, just on a hunch." Poulter shook his doubtfully. "Besides, Byrd himself would veto such a wild-goose chase. Unless . . ."

Poulter grew thoughtful as a thought took form in his mind. One of his long cherished plans was to establish a base some 30 or 40 miles out on the trail from Little America. His idea was to co-ordinate readings with the observatory at Little America. Much additional data could be obtained concerning the behavior of meteors as they plunged from space into the atmosphere of earth. He longed to make these observations before the coming of summer daylight.

If all went well, if the trail were clear, if the tractors behaved properly, if there were not too many crevasses, then why not extend the trip clear to Advance Base? It would be even better as an observation post.

Before Byrd left Little America he had established a kind of constitutional government which was to function in his absence. He had chosen sixteen of the most reliable men. They could, by a two-thirds vote, override any decision made by the "executive branch."

Poulter and Murphy developed their plan, but when they presented it to the camp at large, they ran squarely into firm, steely opposition. For days the tunnels and shacks stormed with argument.

These were men who knew the Barrier, men who knew full well what venturing forth on it at night would mean.

Furthermore, many of them were ex-Navy men who were accustomed to obeying to the letter the orders of their superiors. There was no permission from Byrd to venture forth during the winter. In fact, his final instructions had been brief and most explicit: he had forbidden a night journey in no uncertain terms.

Poulter stood firm on his desire to make the trip in the name of scientific investigation. Murphy on his part, stood just as firm on his intuitions. "I know that a hunch is pretty flimsy stuff to ask men to risk their lives on, but if I should be right, we'd never forgive ourselves."

"This is simply a way to get around a precise order—all this talk about meteors," one of the men said.

"All right, all right," gritted Murphy. "Call it what you like. But I'm going to Advance Base if I have to walk every inch of the way. Byrd is in trouble and I know it."

His vehemence was catching. Doubts formed in many minds. But the answer to the dilemma seemed simple. Why not just ask the man who was supposed to need help? Just put the question to him.

"Never," said Murphy. "I know Byrd and so do you. He'd rather die than let us risk our necks to save him. He couldn't do anything but turn us down."

The argument continued, and raged through long hours. Poulter and Murphy stuck to their guns: as soon as possible make the attempt. It would accomplish two purposes. Poulter would get to look at his meteors, and Murphy would be able to see how Byrd was. Finally the staff gave approval.

It was strictly on the grounds of scientific exploration that the proposed trip was presented and sold to Byrd.

At Advance Base, an exhausted and weary man, worn from his long and bitter struggle, listened incredulously as the calm, logical words poured squawking from his earphones.

He had known about the short base trip Poulter contemplated, but he'd paid little attention to it. His confidence in Poulter and the others was such that he allowed them to plan without comment from him. Aside from his usual injunctions not to take chances with the lives of the men, he had not interfered. But this new idea was something entirely different.

Stunned by the implications, Byrd was unable to reach an immediate decision.

In response to Poulter's courteous, "Well, what do you think?" he had simply tapped out on the key, "Make test runs with the tractors. Let me know the results," and signed off.

This was near the end of June, a whole month since the catastrophe. During this time, by enforcing the most rigorous self-discipline in the use of the stove and by managing his feeble strength like a miser doling out precious jewels, Byrd had progressed, or so he believed. From a state of almost total continuous collapse, there were now short hours when he was "up." Ever so slightly to be sure, but nevertheless, during these times he was able to function more normally.

But now he had to think, to plan, to relate the present to the future. All that afternoon and far into the evening, Byrd sat cross-legged on his bunk, wearily trying to reach a conclusion. With pencil and pad, logarithm tables, Nautical Almanac, a chart of the trail which had been laid out, he groped tiredly through a maze of conflicting facts which governed the feasibility of such a trip.

The difficulties were enormous, and for the most part could only be guessed at. Crevasses. Navigation. Were the orange flags which marked the trail still visible? How about the cold— would it decrease or would it likely get worse? What was the gasoline consumption of the tractors?

As he faced the truly formidable objections, his doubts grew. The surging hope that had sprung to life during the radio contact died and shriveled. Weary and depressed, and completely unable to arrive at a rational answer, he slumped down in the sleeping bag.

Yet, like every man, his hope for life was great. He knew in his heart he would not be able to refuse the permission.

On the next radio schedule, he gave it. Tentative, hedged with restrictions though it was, it nevertheless gave Poulter and his men the right to go ahead. No lives were to be endangered. Poulter was not to strike directly for Advance Base and attempt to reach it by navigation. They must follow the trail of flags.

As June rounded out and the long days started down the slope of July, the cold deepened. Day after day the thermometer slumped into the minus fifties, sixties, and seventies.

The ice in the shack spread slowly higher and higher on the walls. That on the ceiling edged downward to meet it. The floor had long since been a slick, vomit-stained, debris-littered slab.

Topside it seemed to Byrd that the whole world had drawn back on itself, cringing, hoarding its resources. Even the stars which swam their way in ponderous rhythm across the heavens seemed to retreat, to be waiting for the cold to end. Across the deep black flamed the aurora: dazzling, scintillating curtains of light in all colors which rose and fell, twisted and rolled. Their brilliance seemed to intensify the cold.

The Barrier, the ice of the glacier itself, retreated, curling inward, crackling, groaning beneath the cold. Nothing could live, or even exist in the face of such a monstrous enemy. Byrd's life seemed to hang in tenuous balance, fragile. One blow might shatter it.

Then, on July 5, the blow fell.

He started the generator to meet a radio schedule. There was no voltage showing on the meter.

Weakly, his fogged mind almost refused to grapple with such a calamity. He stared at the needle, trying to will it into motion. Impersonally, it hung at zero.

With great deliberations, step by step, he started to track down the fault. Connections, wiring, switches. He worked his way back to the generator itself. The motor was popping away briskly, seemingly without a care in the world, but the generator itself was not turning.

He gave up any idea of meeting the schedule. Calling up all his resources, he dragged the machine painfully into the hut, got it up on the table and started dismantling it.

By supper time he had discovered the fault, and it was fatal. The key, or lug, on the shaft had sheared off—probably crystallized and weakened by the prolonged cold.

He worked steadily, and by midnight the table and the floor were littered with bits and parts. Nothing he could do was of any avail. The only solution was a new shaft, and where on this icy barrier was he to find that?

Despairing, near collapse from weariness, Byrd dragged

himself to the bunk and put out the light. All the sweetness of hope for early relief—the gift of life itself—which had welled up in him was gone. The failure could not have come at a worse time, when communication between Advance Base and Little America was essential.

Too weak even to consider the morning to come and the effort he would have to make to get the emergency transmitter on the air, he finally fell into a nightmarish sleep.

When he awoke, his condition was worse. The long struggle to repair the generator had taken the last of his feeble reserve strength.

Nevertheless, the effort had to be made. He unpacked the emergency generator and transmitter and stood uncertainly, with a great dullness working the cobwebs of his mind. He stared at the inert, neat, gray steel boxes.

Using the instruction booklet he managed to hook the transmitter to the antenna and to make the right connections for power.

The outfit seemed simple and practical, but it was rigged for use by two men. The generator was mounted on a tripod and had two handles, like the pedals on a bicycle, sticking out from its sides, for hand operations. Theoretically, one man cranked and the other worked the sending key. Byrd gave a tentative twist to the cranks. The magnetic drag was not great, but in his condition, it was almost too much.

He checked out the time. He had, of course, missed the regular schedule again, but Dyer had arranged that in the event of a missed contact, he would always listen at two o'clock in the afternoon. It was now one o'clock.

After a meal of hot milk, soup and crackers, Byrd made the first attempt. Slowly winding up the mechanism, cranking with both hands, he got it up to speed. Then with his left hand he tried to keep the generator turning while with his right he attempted to spell out the call letters with the key.

After sending for five minutes—hoping against hope that the signals were getting out and that Dyer was searching the frequency band of the emergency transmitter, he stopped cranking and turned on his own receiver.

Trembling so badly he could scarcely work the dials, he tried to tune in Little America. There was nothing but the scratch and hiss of static, and then, most miraculous of all miracles, Dyer's calm voice floated in out of the darkness. "KFZ to KFY. We hear you KFY. We hear you. Go ahead please."

Shaking with weariness, teeth chattering with cold and with despair, Byrd explained what had happened. He was, he said, "having a bit of trouble managing to crank the generator and send at the same time."

Calm, unhurried, like the trained and studied voice of a police dispatcher, which never betrays excitement or emotion, Dyer replied, "We are sorry to hear this. We understand and will try to keep our messages at a minimum."

Then, speaking also carefully, softly, in quiet tones, Charlie Murphy came on. "If the weather holds clear we shall attempt the meteorological trip near the end of July. Don't expect us before then, and there is a good chance we may be considerably later."

Poulter then gave a resume of the preparations, much of which Byrd missed. His heart was beating like a riveting gun, sending the pulse in liquid thunder through his ears.

Beside Byrd's key was a long list of detailed instructions for the proposed trip and the safety of those who were to embark on it. He sent what he could of the message and then gave out, sagging over the generator.

A very serious group of men gathered in the radio shack at Little America. Dyer had taken off one of the earphones and laid it on the table so that all could hear. Rising, falling, almost incoherent, the thin, far whine of the signal drifted painfully into the radio shack.

It drifted off into unintelligible nothings, paused, and then came in again, went on. Like a thing in despair, this signal seemed surely to reflect the agony of the man on the other end. The code was impersonal, inhuman in itself, yet revealed much in its stumbling.

"Have very thorough drill on trail. Also take more flags," was the gist of the message. Then it was repeated and somehow it seemed like the last testament of a brave man for the welfare of his comrades.

Dyer acknowledged, repeated the message back, but there came no answer. Just the faint, deathly dots and dashes of a sign-off. It sounded like a death knell.

"What do you think, Dyer?" asked Charlie Murphy, but even as he spoke, he knew the answer.

"There's something wrong, Charlie. This isn't just bad sending. This is incoherency."

"I agree," said Poulter.

"Dyer," asked Murphy again, "are those emergency rigs made for two men?"

"Yes. One to crank and one to send."

"But can they be operated by one?"

"Of course. It isn't easy, but if a man—" He broke off.

"But if a man—?" prompted Murphy.

"But if a man is not weakened . . . if he's in full control of himself . . ."

Now Murphy interrupted. "He can do better than that."

Dyer nodded somberly. "Yes, he should be able to do better."

Bit by bit now, the pieces were beginning to drop into place. There was still nothing definite about Byrd, no admission from him that something was wrong, and no real reason for believing it. Nevertheless, Murphy's hunch was beginning to take weight and substance.

At Advance Base, Byrd slumped over the table, utterly wearied by his effort. Although the temperature was 60 degrees below zero, sweat poured from his body, running in dirty rivulets down his chest. But through the dim perception which remained, he found some reason for satisfaction.

His lie was apparently working. At least, the men in Little America did not seem alarmed. The meteor trip as proposed was still a scientific push, well planned and organized, and would be deliberately executed. Nothing he had said or done had seemed to interfere with this. The trip had not degenerated into a frantic rescue attempt, with all its grim potential for real disaster.

Remember to shut off the stove, he stumbled to the sanctuary of the sleeping bag. The effort of this contact had been too much. It very nearly finished him off.

If it had not been for the fuel and food stored in the shack near his bunk for just such an emergency, it is very doubtful whether or not he would have lived over the next few days.

Meantime, Little America launched into full-scale preparations for the trip. Charlie Murphy and Dr. Poulter were not alone now in their concern. Other men also strongly felt this inexplicable twanging of the nerves—this need to make haste.

CHAPTER 14

A TRIP INTO THE NIGHT

AFTER THIS FRIGHTFUL RELAPSE, BYRD WAS AGAIN reduced to a crawling, shambling caricature of a man. Wobbling uncertainly, almost in a daze, he went through the slow-motion efforts to fend off death and to keep contact with Little America.

The meager reserve of strength which he had built up so painfully over the past weeks was completely gone. The precarious mental peace he had won seemed to have vanished. He was easy prey to gloom and despair.

Everything was too much for him. His body rebelled. Sleeplessness returned. Warm cereal or soup or tea, so desperately needed if he were to keep going, came up almost immediately, in retching spasms of uncontrollable nausea. The pains returned—stabbing and rolling in waves of intense agony through his chest and head, leaving him prostrate and drenched with sweat. Gradually, however, by sheer force of will, he drove himself to the point where he could keep down a little food. And with the food, bit by bit his strength seeped back.

When Byrd had gone to Advance Base he weighed about 180 pounds. During this period, he dropped to around 125!

His fingers were raw from touching cold metal. No matter how much food he took or how many clothes he wore it was simply impossible to get the cold out of his body. He was a shivering mass of skin and bones.

So frantic was he for heat, and for light, that against all his resolves, he kept the stove burning longer and longer each day. He even lit the gasoline pressure lamp, soaking up for brief periods the boon of its brilliant light. Again he fell prey to the fumes, but wiser now, he recognized the danger signs, and always shut off the stove in time. So he hung, teetering dangerously on a knife edge, between death from the fumes and death from freezing!

To make matters even worse at this crucial time he again lost contact with Little America. For days, when his strength would permit, he cranked the generator. They never heard him. To make matters doubly painful, his receiver began to go bad. Little America's patient calling, and blind broadcasting had enabled him to keep track somewhat of what was going on, and the friendly voices had cheered him. But now even this was gone.

He dismantled the receiver and the transmitter. For ten days he went through the torture of trying to repair the equipment.

In the receiver he found a loose connection and again he was able to hear Little America.

Fumbling wearily with the transmitter, poring through the instruction booklets, he eventually discovered that one of the leads from the set to the aerial had come loose. To find this simple bad connection had taken him ten days!

The anxious men at Little America were clustered in the radio shack. Hollow-eyed from lack of sleep. Dyer searched the airwaves for Byrd's signal.

The whole noisy world slid beneath his fingers as he twisted the dials. Rome, Paris, London, New York. Ships at sea. But from Advance Base, 123 miles away across the ice to the south, there was only silence. The night was still and empty.

Then suddenly, rising up, swelling in intensity, came the whine of the emergency transmitter. "KFY to KFZ. KFY to KFZ." For five minutes Byrd called them, and then: "k,k,k." The signal to go ahead.

"Good evening Sir. We hear you KFY. Go ahead, please."

The men in the shack slumped with relief as the night was torn by this thin miracle of sound. He was back on the air. Once again, their fears were dissipated. They still had nothing definite to go on. Only the hunch.

Byrd immediately went into a discussion of the instructions he had prepared for Dr. Poulter. Safety. Safety. Above all, safety for the men who were making the trip.

Poulter explained at length the plans and details that had been worked out. They expected to shove off from Little America some time between the 18th and the 23rd of July, weather permitting. This was the period of full moon; its light might possibly spell the difference between success or failure.

July 20. A pale rose glow swung briefly at noon along the horizon and then was drowned in night. The sun, with its life-giving light was on its way back to the Antarctic.

Another contact, which again left Byrd retching and exhausted, informed him that Poulter would leave Little America within the hour. How was the weather at Advance Base? Clear and cold. Byrd's final direct order to the party on the tractor was, "Under no circumstances are you to leave the flagmarked trail."

There was only one thing remaining for him to do to help. Everything else was out of his hands by now. In the blackness of night the tractor party, if it indeed got that far, could pass right by Advance Base without ever seeing it. Beacons of some sort were needed.

Byrd found seven or eight magnesium flares, and he cached them at the foot of the ladder. Then one by one, each an intolerable weight, he carried four empty cans up topside and filled them with gasoline. They would make admirable beacons.

Another brief contact with Little America at midnight. The tractor had started and was reporting progress by radio. The party was having a very rough time. The flags were down and there were many new and dangerous crevasses.

Now began a period of the most intense worry for Byrd. But now the worry was not for himself. Other men, good men, were on the Barrier coming toward him. If they should become lost? The only consolation for him, and it was scant, was that they were not risking death in answer to a plea of his for help. They were coming on business of their own!

Again radio contact was broken. Although he spent long hours once more dismantling the equipment, trying to find out what was wrong, he could neither hear Little America, nor could they hear him.

In final fury, the Barrier unleashed even greater and more terrible weapons. The cold increased. Down, down, down, the thermometer dropped, eventually to reach minus 85 degrees.

Nothing could live on the Barrier in such cold. In desperation Byrd broadcasted, "Poulter, return to Little America. Await warmer weather." The message was never received.

On July 22, as he had done innumerable times since the departure of the tractor, Byrd painfully hoisted himself to the surface and scanned the horizon to the north. Against all hope, all reason, there was always the chance that the yellow glare of the tractor's lights would sweep over the top of some distant ridge of snow. Now and again his heart would leap at a distant bit of light, but always it wavered and faded—an expiring flash of aurora or the beam from a setting star.

Dr. Poulter sat on the hood of the tractor, a searchlight in his hand, trying to find the small orange flags, no bigger than a man's hand. Groping and searching, he strained into the darkness. Each flag was set 293 yards from the last, and he knew, of course, the general bearing of each one, but the task was a difficult one.

The trail had been laid by a dog-sledge party, and although the overall course was accurate, it tended to zig-zag. Dogs never run a true line. They veer off from the beat of the weather and wind and constantly have to be brought back on course by the drivers. Hence, each flag could be as much as 20 or 30 yards off from its true straight-line position.

At last, 50 miles out, the party reached the most difficult part of the journey. An enormous detour had been made to take the trail around an area of impassable crevasses. But from here on the flags were gone, obliterated, blown down during the blizzards. In a last-ditch effort to locate them, the tractor started out in the general direction of the trail, with four men as outriders, on skis. Traveling abreast, 200 yards apart, they searched. There was no use. Not a flag survived. The party returned to the 50-mile depot.

They had come up against a stone wall. Poulter was not able to strike directly into the darkness to navigate a new trail to Advance Base. On the third day, he radioed blind to Byrd: "We are at 50-mile depot unable to locate trail around crevassed area in six hours . . . Think it inadvisable to proceed."

Byrd never got the message.

The men on the tractor had covered 173 miles to make good less than a third of that distance. There was no alternative but to return to Little America.

Byrd was frantic with worry. The cold was unbearable. When he awoke in the morning he could scarcely get out of the sleeping bag. His breath had frozen, congealed. He was nearly encased in ice.

The days passed. Two, three, four, five. Remorse tortured him as his fear mounted that Poulter and his men had met with terrible tragedy. They should have been at Advance Base long ago, or he should have heard from Little America. There was no word. Nothing. Only the impersonal scratching of static and the eternal exhaustion from the futile cranking.

His own hopes died. The spiritual uplift which he had felt at the knowledge his friends were coming was now gone, and with it the will and the strength to hold on.

Nevertheless, he still had his part to play in the scheme, and he must play it to the proper end as long as he was able. He dragged himself out of the sleeping bag and up to the surface to his signal pots. After a dozen faltering attempts, he got a match to the gasoline. The thin columns of black smoke towered into the sky, bending with the wind.

Then he touched off a magnesium flare which was lashed to a bamboo pole. The brilliance blinded him, elbowed the darkness back for a few brief minutes.

There was no answering signal from the north.

The hours after Poulter and his men decided there was no choice but to return to Little America, they were racing one of the worst blizzards of the year. It came without warning, moving like a swift whirling specter across the Barrier.

For a time they tried to force the machine into it, but it was no use. The engine finally stalled as the drift thickened and mounted, reaching the air intake of the carburetor. The motor stopped as if it had been immersed in water.

In a gale of hurricane force, the huge tractor was literally imprisoned in the wind and drift and stinging air. It bucked and lurched for a night and a day. The men huddled in the freezing cabin, trying to stay alive.

When the blizzard finally blew itself out, the weary and

exhausted crew dug the tractor and its trailing sledges out of the snow. After long hours with a blowtorch thawing the frozen engine, they at last got it started and slowly made good the retreat back to Little America. They were guided all the way by a beacon light installed on the top of one of the radio towers.

Contact somehow was miraculously restored with Byrd. The truth of the matter was that his arms had literally given out. There was no more strength left in his muscles to turn the crank. He had managed, however, to rig the generator so that he could crank it with his feet and thus produce a signal that would carry to Little America.

His messages were reassuring, filled with sound advice for the next attempt. There was never in them one word of his own plight. His thoughts and suggestions were invariably for the safety and good of the men who would ride the tractor.

When the contacts were over, his knees knocked together, so violent was his trembling. The nausea mounted again, and with it returned the retching and vomiting that left him weak and helpless. Little America knew nothing about it; his sign-offs always ended with "All okay and cheerio."

However, in spite of all this, fear was mounting and creeping through Little America that Byrd was in real distress. There were the long silences, his troubles with the radio equipment. The pauses, some of them minutes long between words. When asked about the hesitation and the silences, Byrd casually said he had a "bad arm," which made cranking difficult.

In any event, Dr. Poulter decided to ignore the instructions to stick to the marked trail. He would make a direct run for

Advance Base by the stars. There were no opposing voices now. The dark suspicions had permeated the entire camp.

He reduced his crew to three—fewer supplies would have to be carried and perhaps they could make better time. The weather turned bad again and the party was a prisoner of the wind, cold and ice.

On August 2 a feeble call came out of the darkness to the south. "Where is tractor? Have heard nothing for days."

Dyer managed to establish the contact, and the new plans were revealed to Byrd. Poulter was very careful to say nothing that would give Byrd any suspicion that Little America was concerned about him. They knew that if he thought the tractor trip was anything like a rescue attempt, with all the fearful dangers involved, he would veto it.

Byrd replied: "Can hear only a few words. I have lights outside from 3 to 8 p.m. Everything okay here. Good luck."

CHAPTER 15

RESCUE ACCOMPLISHED

ANXIOUS DAYS PASSED. SPRING WAS COMING, AND ITS presence was announced each morning by the slowly increasing light on the horizon. First it was a vague gray, then as the stars spun ponderously through their orbits, each day the light increased, taking on faint rosy hues, greens, violets. Each day the "sunrise" lasted a little longer before it was gone, and night again fell.

Time for Byrd had frozen. It no longer moved. There was only the painful present through which he must live. Every ounce of his strength went into the effort to keep communications open. He grew to hate the radio with a feeling so strong that at times he could scarcely keep from smashing it to bits.

But crank he must, as long as he could. The effort drained

him more and more each time. Each time he recovered more and more slowly. Nevertheless, the job had to be done. It was essential to Poulter to know the state of weather at Advance Base. Byrd had to know their plans so he could light his signal beacons at the proper times.

On August 4, Poulter left Little America again and ran into difficulties immediately. The blizzard had destroyed more trail flags. Probing blindly to the east he and his men ran into a huge, unsuspected area of crevasses. A bridge over one of them let go. Rather than jump in an effort to save himself, the driver took the chance and hit the gas, clawing his way out, but leaving behind a gaping hole in which the trailing sledges carrying food and equipment dangled. Several hours were lost getting the expedition on the move again.

The fact that Poulter was actually heading south once more penetrated through Byrd's dullness of spirit. Hope once again buoyed him to make the effort to live and to do what must be done.

Knowing only that the tractor had started but having no way to know where it was or when it might arrive at Advance Base, Byrd did his part in lighting the flares and beacons by guess-work. After each time he tiredly searched the horizon to the north. There was only black emptiness and again the worry commenced. Again he berated himself for allowing the men to start out.

On the third day, Poulter informed Little America that the clutch was gone on the tractor and they would have to return.

He requested that the crews have No. 3 tractor warmed, fueled and ready to go.

The order had been anticipated. It was already on the ramp, engine thawed and turning over.

Poulter and his men arrived, frozen to the bone, and weary. After talking it over, they decided not to use No. 3. This machine had caught fire the summer before and had never been thoroughly reconditioned. The remaining tractor had not been repaired at all and was completely unfit for the trail.

They decided to replace the broken clutch with one from one of the other tractors, but cruelly, it wouldn't fit. It became necessary to cannibalize all the machines in order to get No. 3 in condition. The instrument panel was changed, headlights were installed, and other repairs were made.

The voice welled out of the north into the dim shadows of the hut at Advance Base. "Dick," said Charlie Murphy, "Poulter is back in Little America. The clutch broke down on the tractor." He went on to explain reasonably what had happened and that the crew would put out again as soon as possible.

And then, driven by a violent urge to know the truth, breaking the resolve made over and over to himself not to touch the point, Murphy put the fateful question: "Dick, the truth is, we are more than worried about you. Are you ill? Are you hurt?" Murphy's tone was flat, conversational. It carried not a hint of the depth of his concern.

There was a long pause. Perhaps it was intentional, or perhaps it was just one of the breaks to which they had become accustomed. Then Byrd: "I understand about the tractor. Now, since you will be navigating . . ." The message trailed off into incoherencies, stumbling, weaving, hesitating.

Dyer's typewriter tried to keep up but finally it stopped. This was hardly code at all. It was approaching gibberish. To Murphy it seemed a cry of pain.

Murphy went on the air again. Insisting on an answer. "Tell me what's wrong, Dick? Do you want Poulter to bring Dr. Potaka?"

Another long hesitation, another long faltering wait while the wind rustled in the ventilators and the very Barrier seemed to creak and groan under its intolerable burden of ice and cold.

Then clearly, crisply, the whine of the generator rose again from Advance Base. "No doctor. Nothing to worry about . . ." A long pause. "Only please don't ask me to crank any more."

And there it was. No longer any need for anyone to guess. Murphy had been right. There was trouble, serious trouble at Advance Base. Not an admission, not a plea—just the simple statement: "Don't ask me to crank any more."

Very very carefully, so as not to give away a bit of his feelings, understanding well what Byrd's reaction would be if he suspected they had pierced his evasion, Murphy said quietly: "We appreciate how hard the cranking must be. Don't worry about us or Poulter. See you on the air tomorrow."

All the speculation, all the doubt, was now gone. Little America threw its entire resources into a desperate effort to get the tractor away.

At 1:20 in the morning it rolled, like a slothful, ungainly, unwieldy monster across the white snow, gleaming dully in the light of an orange-blue moon.

An hour later it was back. The oil pump had given up. The engine was in danger of burning out.

How long it stayed nobody knew. They didn't keep track of time at a moment like this. And now, they berated themselves, for the facts had been clear as crystal from the very beginning. Little America was the victim of a conspiracy. Their awareness had been blunted by the cold and the darkness. Byrd's insistence that all was well had lulled them. But the evidence had been there if they had only been able to see it. All of it.

All hands worked on the balky tractor, and eventually it got away again. With the engine roaring wide open, spewing steam from the exhaust into the air, the big machine lumbered away to the southward. The hearts and prayers of everyone at Little America rolled with it.

By the following evening Poulter and his men were a bit over 50 miles out—at the same spot where they had previously been stopped dead by the crevasses.

Abandoning the flag trail now, they headed out in a wide detour around the rolling depression. They steered entirely by compass. To help with the navigation, Dr. Poulter built behind them small snow beacons on which he stuck perforated tin cans containing candles or flashlights. By these dim pinpoints of lights, they were able to make reasonably straight runs.

The long hours wore on. The work was heartbreakingly slow but there could be no other way. To become hopelessly lost would mean disaster. Worst of all, the cold was again deepening.

At Advance Base, Byrd miserably contemplated about him the evidence of his ruin. Books had tumbled from the shelves—he had no strength to pick them up. Frozen, half-eaten cans of food were everywhere. The parts of the generator lay scattered in disorderly confusion. Frozen filth covered the floor, was in the slop pails. The ice now had completely encircled the walls and ceiling. There was nothing left now for the Barrier to conquer except the will of the man who still struggled, who was still alone.

But his situation was not one of total collapse yet. The spirit and the animal-like determination to live still burned in him. And greatest of all boons to the human heart, the darkness was going. Each day the sun lifted itself a bit closer to the horizon, suffusing the dark for brief minutes with bright banners of light. In less than three weeks the sun would heave itself into the sky, and then, higher and higher, and for a longer and longer time each day. Spring would have come to the Antarctic.

So Byrd's morale improved in spite of his increasing physical deterioration. This time he was realistic. No false hopes. No heart-wrenching agony at the thought of failure of the party coming toward him. Out of a vast and painfully learned humility, he had become convinced of his own small value. Compared to it, the success of the expedition and the safety of the men on the tractor were paramount. If they reached him in time—fine. If not, there was little he could do, or wanted to do. The issue was almost out of his hands.

Almost out of his hands—but not entirely. The lights and signal flares must be tended as agreed. He had prepared additional fire and smoke pots which were stacked at the foot of the ladder leading topside. By exerting himself to the fullest, he was able to make one trip an hour up and down the ladder, with one can at a time. Finally they were topside and filled with gasoline. He also carried up more magnesium flares and a signal kite. This was all he could do to help, and in a very real sense, it was his last stand.

These simple preparations, weakening as they were, helped to clear his mind and set his conscience at rest. There was nothing more that he could do. His great fear was of another blizzard, which would surely mean the end for him and for the meteor party.

The weather remained clear. One day passed. A difficult radio contact with Little America left him weak, shaking, too shattered even to be cheered by the news that Poulter was still on his way, making good time. The final admonition from the base: "Dick, don't neglect the lights."

"Don't neglect the lights." It was a catch phrase to keep him on his feet. Poulter could easily miss Advance Base in the night by a distance of a few yards. Once having overshot, the difficulties of ever finding it would be enormously increased.

Another day passed. Byrd awoke with a violent start, the warning still ringing in his ears. If Poulter had not met with disaster, he could even now be near Advance Base, searching and probing in the blackness.

Weakly, Byrd dressed as fast as he could, lit the stove, and crept topside. He scanned the horizon and the sky. No sign of searchlights. Only the glittering stars. Then, before his astonished eyes, a feeble yellow glow seemed to lift a moment and then creep waveringly along the dim line that separated ice from sky.

He hauled the kite up the ladder with a string and soaked the long tail in gasoline. He left a couple of feet of dry paper at the end to serve as a sort of fuse.

Carrying the kite, he started downwind, crawling part way. He stuck it upright in the snow and lit the tail. Then stumbling through the darkness, he went back to the ball of string as quickly as possible. It was out of the question for him to run to get the kite aloft, so he hauled on the cord with all his strength. The kite took off beautifully, soaring straight up into the starlit sky, the tail burning like a fiery meteor.

When it burned out he lit the gasoline pots and set off a flare. The dazzling blue and white flame vanquished for a few minutes the velvety blackness.

There was no response from the north. In a frenzy of hope he had wasted valuable signals and squandered his strength. The wavering light he had seen was only a star. Poulter was still too far off to see the flares, which certainly must have been visible for 20 miles. Hope died and once more Byrd forced himself to be coldly realistic. Perhaps Poulter was nowhere out there at all.

That night there was another radio contact with Little America. Murphy was jubilant. Poulter had stopped the tractor long enough to keep a radio schedule. The party was 91 miles out. With luck they should be at Advance base early in the morning.

The possibility was almost too great for Byrd's mind to grasp. Could it really be true? Driving his mind mercilessly to obedience, he forced the hope and optimism down.

Nevertheless, at five in the morning, he was up on the Barrier. The brief gray dawn light flickered and vanished. Never had the Barrier seemed colder, more empty, more dangerous.

To the best of men, the healthiest, the most cheerful, the

darkness of dawn is apt to be a time of uncertainty, of depression. This morning it brought to Byrd a despair beyond any telling. Nevertheless, he lit a can of gasoline. There was no answer, nor did he expect any.

He went below again, took a little hot milk and a short rest. At six he was up again at the trapdoor, anxiously scanning the northern horizon.

This time, again, he seemed to see something. A thin yellow, beam, which could be from a searchlight, seemed to lift from the Barrier, flicker across the sky, then die.

He made for the kite, half falling, in a stumbling run. Making a flare fast to the tail, he repeated the maneuver of the previous morning. When the flare died out, blackness plunged down again like a stone. There was no answer. No finger of light lanced to the sky.

This was the 71st day since Byrd's collapse. He had endured as much as a human being could absorb. Convinced that the light he had seen was only an hallucination, he slumped in the snow, then crawled to the hatch, slid down the ladder and fell in his bunk.

Yet he could not lie still. In spite of himself, hope had risen strongly and would not be silenced. By seven o'clock he was again on the Barrier. Nothing to the north. Even the stars were gone, obscured in black and ominous clouds. He lit another flare, two more pots of gasoline. Still the empty darkness.

Again, below, he stood reeling in the middle of the littered, frozen room. The red tracing on the thermograph had started down again, was far into the minus forties. Bitter cold, and perhaps with it, would come the bitter end of his hopes.

Byrd's mind turned vague, fuzzy. He was fast reaching his very limit. He passed out, and when he was roused by the cold he found he was sprawled half in and half out of his bunk. He pulled himself into his sleeping bag, past caring what happened. An hour and a half later he awakened, his mind cleared by the brief rest. The lights must be tended!

He forced himself up the ladder; suddenly his strength drained out of him completely. He plunged back down to the ice below.

He obviously needed some kind of a stimulant if he were going to do his job. Once before he had tried a half-glass of alcohol. He had been ill for days from it. Desperately he rummaged in the medicine kit, and came across a bottle of hypophosphate containing strychnine. Strychnine! That might do the trick. The dosage was one teaspoon in a cup of water. The fluid in the bottle was frozen but he thawed it and took three teaspoons in water, followed by three cups of the strongest tea he could brew.

Lightheaded and dizzy, he nevertheless found strength pouring into his body. He went up the ladder and examined the sky. To the north there was nothing but clouds. Beneath them the white of the Barrier was an interminable dull gleam. He threw a wire over the radio antenna, tied one of the flares to it, in the fuse, and hauled it up. He had strength to spare for the moment.

The blinding glare knifed the darkness. When it died, Byrd peered. And there it was! A finger of light answered—waving and trembling across the sky.

He sat down, forced himself to look to the south, to the

opposite horizon. Then he turned, fortifying himself against disappointment, but there was no mistake.

As nearly as he could judge the tractor was five or ten miles away. It could not be at Advance Base for another hour or two.

Byrd went below, intending to clean up the shack, ashamed to have his friends see the evidence of his frailty. He made a few feeble stabs at the mess and then gave up. The miracle of life was all that mattered. Before this gift, shame dwindled to nothing.

He hacked three cans of soup into a pan with a hammer, and put them on the stove to heat. There at least must be warm food for his guests.

Going back up, he lit more flares, more smoke pots. The welcoming lights of the tractor approached nearer and nearer until at last he could hear the crunch of the treads on the snow and the beep-beep of its horn.

As a greeting he set off the last of the flares. Its light was dying when the car stopped, its clatter and rumble stilled, a hundred yards away.

He stood up, but did not dare walk toward the three men hurrying toward him.

The still burning lights of the tractor picked up a fur-clad figure standing, waiting. "Hello, fellows. Come on down. I have a bowl of hot soup waiting for you."

The pattern was at least complete. The final piece of the jigsaw had dropped into place, neatly fitting into the whole, placed there by the enduring worth of a man, of his honor, of his responsibility toward his fellows.

The dignity of a human being was well guarded during the two months of Byrd's convalescence at Advance Base. The private places in our spirits from which spring our individuality and our personal worth were well guarded. Byrd never mentioned the true depths of his weakness and collapse. And Poulter and his men, even with the evidence of the ruin about them, the notes stuck on a nail over the bunk, kept their own thoughts and did not press him to reveal fully the details of his trial.

Thus on August 11, 1934, ended the personal saga of a great man.

On October 14, in full daylight, a powerful expedition stood poised in Little America, waiting to go. It waited only for Byrd's arrival and the wisdom of his leadership.

The plane arrived to take him from Advance Base. He climbed into the hatch and never looked back. "Part of me remained forever at 80 degrees 8 minutes South: what survived of my youth, my vanity perhaps, and certainly my skepticism. On the other hand I did take away something which I had not fully possessed before: appreciation of the sheer beauty and the miracle of being alive, and a humble set of values ... I live more simply now, and with more peace."

So ended Richard Evelyn Byrd's greatest assault—the conquering of himself. It is a strange document, one of the most personal, most revealing stories ever written about a man. Alone, in quiet and dark despair, he was given the opportunity to pass the ultimate test, and he did not fail.

CHAPTER 16

A PRICELESS
CONTRIBUTION

MR. POULTER'S TRIBUTE TO BYRD, PERHAPS THE greatest which a scientist can make, was the simple statement: "All the meteorological records were complete."

For the first time in history correlated weather readings had been made in the Antarctic. It was a priceless contribution. The fact that it was available at all was a miracle—complete proof of Byrd's dedication, and his will to complete what he set out to do.

But the weather data was only a part of the rich material assembled by the expedition during the spring and summer. The field parties gathered enormously valuable information of many diverse kinds. All of it shed light on the unknown and opened up to man additional glimpses of the mysteries of the Antarctic.

The *Bear* and the *Jacob Ruppert* arrived on schedule and by

February 7, 1935, they were loaded and on their way home. To further extend the mapping, Byrd kept the ships in the Ross Sea until literally the last moment. The sea-smoke was drifting across the water and pancake ice was already forming when they sailed for home.

Once more the continent lived in solitude, alone but for the brief visits of whales, seals, and swooping skua gulls. Soon these also would be gone and Antarctica would be deep in the grip of winter. It would exist only for the men in their memory.

On May 10 the telegraph rang from the bridge: "Finished With Engines." The pulse of life and power died from the *Ruppert*. She was home.

Byrd stepped on the dock to be welcomed by President Franklin D. Roosevelt and to receive from him personally the thanks of the United States government and its people.

But the lure of the South was strong. The call of the goddess of the Antarctic could not go unheeded. Never, during the rest of his life, was Byrd to be free of its magic spell.

Scarcely had he finished paying all the debts incurred by the expedition than he was deep in the planning for another trip.

In 1939, at the age of 51, once more Byrd was heading southward. Only this time, the financing of the expedition was on more powerful shoulders than his own. The importance of the Antarctic could no longer be overlooked. The work which he had accomplished revealed some of the wonders of the great continent, but it only scratched the surface. The need for more knowledge was now widely recognized. The well-equipped expedition he commanded was sponsored by the government—

the United States Antarctic Service had been established under the Department of the Interior.

Little America III was set up, as well as another base, far to the east, on the Palmer Peninsula. The old dream of Haines and Byrd—correlated observations—had really come true.

With World War II imminent, the expedition was called home in 1941.

During the war, Admiral Byrd, back on active duty now, performed extremely valuable and highly confidential tasks. In a way, his work was still that of an explorer, a geographer. He set up a series of Naval and bomber bases through the islands of the South Pacific and then developed the plans for supplying them. He was reminded of the planning and the logistics of his Polar expeditions: First find your bases, then plan how you are going to maintain them, keeping in mind always the cardinal condition: everything must be brought from home, except the air you breathe!

The end of the war brought changes to Admiral Byrd, but in one thing, there was no change. His heart and his soul longed for the icy wastes of Antarctica. In his mind's eye he could see the endless sweep of the Barrier, the lofty mountains, the sky crawling with stars and slashed by the flames of the aurora. He seemed to hear the lonely howling of the Huskies, felt the clean bite of the cold on his body, its stinging, rich air in his lungs. There was no denying the call.

Once more, he was on a ship whose keel slid to the south. This time he was in command of a mighty armada—Operation "Highjump," of the United States Navy. It comprised planes, helicopters, 12 ships and over 4,000 men, and was to make a powerful assault on the continent. The fleet was under the operational command of Rear Admiral Richard H. Cruzen, who had accompanied Byrd as an ice-breaker commander on the Antarctic Service Expedition.

As Byrd stood on the deck watching the coast of the United States swiftly vanishing astern his thoughts must have turned with deep emotion and nostalgia back to other days. Days when the *City of New York*, the *Eleanor Bolling*, the *Bear of Oakland* and the *Jacob Ruppert*, groaning under enormous loads of equipment, had stumbled falteringly through the same seas—southbound.

He also must have thought of the good comrades of those days—Gould, Poulter, Balchen, Haines, Siple, June, Murphy and many many others.

When Little America—this time christened Little America the IVth—was again inhabited, he must have wandered through the icy tunnels and peered into the dingy shacks with something more than a twist in his heart. Here were spent the days of his young manhood; here had been the scene of his own personal battles and hopes and dreams. And here . . . here was the radio shack, small and darkened, in which the desperate vigil had been kept and the evasions planned, the "lies" executed which were to save his life as he lay dying at Advance Base.

And then he must have thought . . . never, have I been truly alone. Always about him were good comrades, good men. Even now, on this expedition, twelve of his old timers were with him.

So great was Byrd's enormous magnetism, the spark of his personality, the attraction which this quiet, honest man had on others, that whenever the news got around that Byrd was heading south again, the veterans drifted back to him. Or perhaps it was something else that called them. Perhaps they, too, like their old commander, also heard the call of the Antarctic and could do no more than answer.

On this expedition, Byrd made his second flight across the South Pole. As the powerful modern plane swept without any struggle high over the glaciers, he must have remembered Liv's glacier. How could he ever forget Bernt Balchen fighting by sheer force of will to lift the stumbling old Ford tri-motor over the crest? How not to see again in his mind's eye the last bag of food flying out the trapdoor to burst on the ice below them? The old days . . . the days of youth had been wonderful days . . .

But these were great times too. The expedition was equipped with all the marvelous devices developed during the War—radar, JATO, powerful new cameras, the latest in electronic navigation devices, fuels and lubricants especially designed for use in Polar regions—and many more.

Byrd and his veterans directed all the flights and sledge trips. Their wise and experienced counsel was invaluable. They comprised a cadre of people with more experience in this field than any other living group of men.

Vast areas, enormous lengths of coastline, mountain ranges, archipelagoes, and seas were discovered, mapped and charted accurately.

In 1952, when plans for the International Geophysical Year were formulated, Byrd's reports and recommendations took full effect. Sixty-four nations would participate, and the program included establishment of Antarctic bases.

Now Byrd heeded for the last time the call of the Antarctic. In command of America's participation in the IGY program, he headed south. Once more he was on a ship heading for the southern oceans.

In 1957, Little America V was established and plans were made for setting up of other bases even further toward the Pole. And, shades of Advance Base—a permanent Base was established right on the Pole itself! The comfort, the facilities, the scientific apparatus of this expedition were a far cry from those of the rude hut which had nearly taken Byrd's life 23 years back. The new Advance Base was commanded by one of Byrd's old men—Paul Siple—now a mature responsible scientist. No better man could have been found.

With the expedition finally established, Byrd returned home to the States to plan the final scientific aspects of the program.

On March 11, 1957, the last report was done. The last phase of the projected work had been planned out to the final detail. The paper work, which Byrd always hated but from which he could never seem to escape, was done. Soon he would be heading back to Antarctica.

That night, in his sleep, he died, at the age of 69.

Byrd may be the last of the great terrestrial explorers. The unknown places on our earth have been reduced to the vanishing point. Only the Antarctic remains, and it, too, had been assaulted so persistently and so violently that it is slowly yielding to man's indomitable restlessness. The Antarctic has long resisted—for various reasons. Surrounded by stormy seas, defended by ramparts of steely ice, impassable mountains, and offering little of immediate commercial value, it has been the last unknown continent in our conquest of the globe on which we live.

Since Byrd's expedition, man has ventured into outer space and to the moon—far beyond the atmosphere of our mother planet.

But wherever man goes, he will not be required to have greater heart than those who breached the frozen southern continent. And of all those—none were of a higher order than Richard Byrd.

Surely somewhere young people today are dreaming and looking at the stars just as Dick Byrd did when he was a small boy. Here are his words about those dreams, and they apply just as much now as they did when he had them and when he wrote of them. They are the words of a courageous adventurer, but they are also the words of a poet:

"When I was growing up I used to steal out of the house at night and go walking. In the heavy shadows of the Shenandoah woods the darkness was terrifying, as it is to all small boys. But when I would pause and look up, a feeling that was midway between peace and exhilaration would seize me. I never succeeded in analyzing that feeling . . . as a boy, as a naval officer, and later, as an explorer when I looked upon mountains and lands which no one before me had ever seen. No doubt it was partly animal—the sheer expanding joy of being alive, of growing, of no longer being afraid. But there was more to it than just that. There was the sense of identification with vast movements: the premonition of destiny that is implicit in every man: the sense of waiting for the momentary revelation"

Index

ABOUT THE AUTHOR

PAUL RINK had a natural interest in the life and adventures of Admiral Byrd. Both were Naval officers, both had a strong interest in science, both had a wanderlust and both felt a need to write.

Rink was born in San Jose, California, attended the California Maritime Academy and the Inter-American University in Panama. He spent seven years in South America, working in the fields of mechanical and steam engineering, physics, and electronics. During WWII he did intelligence work in Central America and then went to sea. He wound up as an Engineering Officer on an Army transport in the South Pacific.

After his days at sea, Paul Rink devoted himself to writing. In addition to his many books for young readers, he published articles in *American Heritage* and *Esquire*. Among the dramatizations he wrote for television was an episode for the popular show "Bonanza".

BOOKS IN THIS SERIES

George Washington: Frontier Colonel
BY STERLING NORTH

John Paul Jones: The Pirate Patriot
BY ARMSTRONG SPERRY

The Stout-Hearted Seven:
Orphaned on the Oregon Trail
BY NETA LOHNES FRAZIER

Geronimo: Wolf of the Warpath
BY RALPH MOODY

Lawrence of Arabia
BY ALISTAIR MACLEAN

Admiral Richard Byrd: Alone in the Antarctic
BY PAUL RINK

General George Patton: Old Blood & Guts
BY ALDEN HATCH

The Sinking of the Bismarck:
The Deadly Hunt
BY WILLIAM SHIRER